W9-DCL-419

Date: 6/4/19

200.223 DOW
Dowley, Tim,
Atlas of world religions /

PALM BEACH COUNTY
LIBRARY SYSTEM
3650 SUMMIT BLVD.
WEST PALM BEACH, FL 33406

ATLAS OF WORLD RELIGIONS

Also in this series

Atlas of Christian History: Tim Dowley, 2016

Atlas of the European Reformations: Tim Dowley, 2015

Atlas of World Religions

by Tim Dowley

Cartographer Nick Rowland FRGS

Fortress Press
Minneapolis

ATLAS OF WORLD RELIGIONS

Copyright © 2018 Fortress Press / ZipAddress Limited. All rights reserved. Except for brief quotations in critical articles or reviews, no part of this book may be reproduced in any manner without prior written permission from the publisher. Email copyright@1517media or write to Permissions, Fortress Press, PO Box 1209, Minneapolis, MN 55440-1209

The right of Tim Dowley to be identified as the author of this work has been asserted by him.

Cover design: Alisha Lofgren

Print ISBN: 978-1-4514-9968-1
eBook ISBN: 978-1-5064-3975-4

The paper used in this publication meets the minimum requirements of American National Standard for Information Sciences — Permanence of Paper for Printed Library Materials, ANSI Z329.48-1984.

Manufactured in the USA

18 19 20 21 22   9 8 7 6 5 4 3 2 1

Photograph acknowledgements
Dreamstime.com:
pp. 14–15 and cover © Onefivenine
p. 26 and cover © Alexandre Fagundes De Fagundes
pp. 32–33 and cover, p. 125 © Pniesen
p. 38 © Kshishtofp
p. 42 and cover © Kalcutta
pp. 44–45 and cover © Sudhir0602
p. 54 © Yamitato
p. 56 and cover © Sean Pavone
pp. 58–59 © Lamzin Vladimir Lamzin Vladimir
p. 72 © Alan Kolnik
pp. 80–81 and cover © Kobby Dagan
p. 82 © Yoav Sinai
p. 96 © Checco
p. 107 © Ken Wolter
pp. 108–109 © Ahmad Faizal Yahya
p. 114 and cover © Konstantin Kaltygin
p. 124 © Marta Beckett
pp. 132–33 © Chalermphon Kumchai
p. 141 © Hoang Bao Nguye
p. 148 © Joserpizarro

Religion indeed enlightens, terrifies, subdues;
it gives faith, it inflicts remorse, it inspires resolutions,
it draws tears, it inflames devotion…

JOHN HENRY NEWMAN (1801–90)

Contents

List of Maps

This atlas aims to survey the origins, historical development, and current strength, distribution, and nature of the major world religions and their offshoots, and to look at some of the religions of the ancient world. To do this within a relatively short book, it has been necessary to be selective in the choice of topics and periods covered. For instance, there is no treatment of Judaism in the medieval period, as this is fully covered in the companion volume, *Atlas of Christian History*. Important aspects of history of the church – such as the development of monasticism, the power and size of the church and the papacy in the High Middle Ages, detailed treatment of the Protestant and Catholic Reformations, and the religious wars that followed – are also treated comprehensively in *Atlas of Christian History*, and it was felt otiose to duplicate coverage in this book.

The text accompanying the maps is not intended to provide exhaustive coverage of the history and development of world religions, but offers an accessible commentary to aid understanding and interpretation of the respective maps.

The various sections of the book are arranged broadly in chronological order of the founding or origins of the religions. A timeline is also provided to give useful chronological comparisons of their history and development.

Tim Dowley
Dulwich, January 2017

A Chronology of World Religions

Mesopotamia

2800–2350 BCE	Sumerian city states
2360–2180	Akkadian Empire, Mesopotamia
1450 BCE	Rise of Assyria
745–727	Tiglath-Pileser III
705–681 BCE	Sennacherib

Egypt

2700–2200 BCE	Egypt: Old Kingdom – Pyramid Age
r. 1545–1525 BCE	Amen-hotep I
r. 1515–1495 BCE	Thutmose I
1290–24 BCE	Ramses II

Hinduism

c. 2700 BCE	Harappa Culture in Indus Valley
c. 800 BCE	Oral *Vedas* collected
c. 600 BCE	*Upanishads* collected
c. 200 BCE–200 CE	*Bhagavad Gita* collected
c. 200 BCE	First contacts with South-east Asia
c. 50 CE	Tantric tradition begins
1000–1150	Angkor Wat built in Cambodia
1948 CE	Mohandas [Mahatma] Gandhi assassinated
1998	Hindu nationalist party BJP wins Indian election

Zoroastrianism

628–551 BCE	Zoroaster
205–276 CE	Mani
651 CE	End of Persian Empire

Buddhism

c. 563–483 BCE	Siddhartha Gautama, the Buddha (traditional dates)
c. 395 BCE	First Buddhist Council, Vaisali
c. 272–232 BCE	r. Ashoka, Indian king who spread Buddhism
c. 100 BCE	Indian Mahayana Buddhism emerges
c. 50 CE	Buddhism enters China
220 CE	First Buddhist mission to Vietnam
372	Buddhism enters Korea from China
c. 552 CE	Buddhism enters Japan
c. 630 CE	Buddhism enters Tibet
c. 745 CE	Buddhists persecuted in China
805 CE	Saicho founds Tendai school
806 CE	Kukai founds Shingon school
845 CE	Buddhists persecuted in China
c. 1000	Theravada Buddhism revives in Sri Lanka and S. E. Asia
1175	Honen founds Pure Land sect
1253	Nichiren founds Nichiren sect
c. 1200	Zen starts to grow in China, spreads to Japan
c. 1617	Dalai Lamas become rulers of Tibet
1952	World Fellowship of Buddhists starts
1959	China takes over Tibet: suppresses Buddhism
1989	Dalai Lama awarded Nobel Peace Prize

Jainism

c. 527, 510 or 425 BCE	Death of Mahaviri (by tradition)
466 or 453 BCE	Council at Valabhi: Shvetamabara fixed
c. 350 BCE	Split between Digambara and Shvetambara
C17	Shvetambara Sthanakvasi sect begins
C18	Shvetambara Terapanth sect begins
1949	Jain World Mission founded

Sikhism

1469–1539 CE	Nanak, founder of Sikhism
1603–4 CE	Adi Granth compiled
1666–1708	Gobind Singh
1695	*Khalsa* formed
1799	Punjab united under Ramjit Singh
1984	Indian government expels militants from Golden Temple, Amritsar, killing many Sikhs

Taoism & Confucianism

c. 600–500 BCE	Legendary Lao Tsu
c. 551–479 BCE	Confucius
c. 630 CE	All Chinese provinces to honour Confucius
1445 CE	Taoist canon published
1949	Communists take over mainland China

Shinto

c. 660 BCE	Legendary Emperor Jimmu
1868 CE	Rule of Emperor Meiji begins
1882	State Shinto begins
1945	State Shinto ends
1946	Emperor Hirohito rejects divine title

Judaism

c. 1800 BCE	Traditional date of patriarch Abraham
c. 1250 BCE	Traditional date of Exodus from Egypt
1200–1020 BCE	'Judges' rule Israel
c. 1160 BCE	Philistines settle Palestine coast
c. 1000–961 BCE	King David
c. 950 BCE	Solomon's Temple built
922 BCE	Israel divides into Northern and Southern Kingdoms (Israel and Judah)
722 BCE	Assyria conquers Northern Kingdom
586–539 BCE	Solomon's Temple destroyed; Exile to Babylonia
520–515 BCE	Second Temple built
166–160 BCE	Maccabean Rebellion
r. 40–4 BCE	Herod the Great
70 CE	Herod's Temple destroyed
c. 400 CE	Palestinian Talmud completed
c. 600 CE	Babylonian Talmud completed
1492 CE	Jews expelled from Spain
c. 1698–1759	*Baal Shem Tov* in Poland
c. 1800 CE	Reform movement spreads in Western Europe
1897	First Zionist Congress
1938–1945	Jewish Holocaust
1948	State of Israel founded

Christianity

4 BCE–30 CE	Jesus of Nazareth
c. 65 CE	Apostle Paul dies
312 CE	Emperor Constantine recognizes Christianity
325	First Council of Nicaea
335	Constantine builds Church of the Holy Sepulchre, Jerusalem

431	Council of Ephesus condemns Nestorianism
451	Council of Chalcedon
476	Fall of Roman Empire in West
529	Benedict establishes his first monastery
862	Cyril and Methodius' mission to Moravia
1054	Great Schism
1095	First Crusade called
1123	First Lateran Council
1176	Carthusian monastic order established
1517	Beginning of Protestant Reformation
1549	Francis Xavier reaches Japan
1563	Council of Trent ends
1611	King James Version of Bible
1738	John Wesley's conversion experience
1795	London Missionary Society founded
1799	Church Missionary Society founded
1804	British & Foreign Bible Society founded
1830	Book of Mormon
1895	World Student Christian Federation founded
1948	First assembly of World Council of Churches
1962–65	Second Vatican Council

Islam

570–632 CE	Prophet Muhammad
622 CE	Hijra: Muhammad's flight from Mecca to Medina
630	Conquest of Mecca
634–35	Conquest of Jordan, Palestine, Syria, Lebanon, Persia
641–43	Conquest of Egypt, Libya, Carthage, Nubia
732	Battle of Poitiers stops Muslim expansion to France
705–715	Conquest of Central Asia, Sind, Spain
1058–1111	Sufi scholar al-Ghazali
1291	Muslims expel Crusaders from Palestine
1492	Muslims expelled from Spain
1529	Otttoman Turks reach Vienna
1526–1857	Mughal Empire, India
1947	Islamic state of Pakistan formed
1979	Islamic Revolution, Iran
2001	Islamist terrorists attacks in USA

Part 1

The Ancient World

Megaliths

Towards the end of the Neolithic era megaliths – structures composed of large stones – were erected in Europe. Most were dolmens – burial structures consisting of a large, flat stone supported on uprights, and passage graves – located on islands and shores of the Mediterranean and western Europe.

However, as well as these megalithic tombs, there were menhirs – huge alignments of stones – such as those at Carnac, Brittany. Their purpose is unknown; possibly they marked ritual procession routes.

Some large constructions, such as the Hal Tarxien stone buildings in Malta, were apparently temples: chalk sculptures found in them display realistic human features, and may represent gods and goddesses and their priests.

Other megalithic structures possibly had astronomical functions, perhaps to help farmers determine the calendar and agricultural seasons. For instance, Stonehenge, on Salisbury Plain, England, has a circle of sarsen stones, some of which line up with the sunrise at midsummer. Whatever its calendar purpose, Stonehenge was also a place of worship; archaeologists have suggested that fertility-gods and goddesses were worshipped there.

THE MEGALITHS OF WESTERN EUROPE

map 1

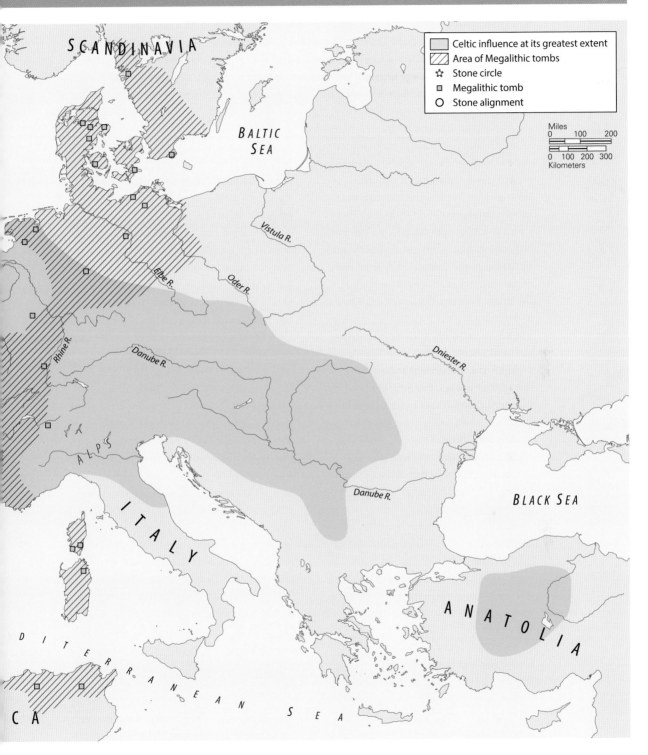

Celtic influence at its greatest extent
Area of Megalithic tombs
☆ Stone circle
▫ Megalithic tomb
○ Stone alignment

SCANDINAVIA

BALTIC SEA

Miles
0   100   200
0 100 200 300
Kilometers

Vistula R.

Elbe R.

Oder R.

Dniester R.

Rhine R.

Danube R.

ALPS

Danube R.

BLACK SEA

ITALY

ANATOLIA

MEDITERRANEAN SEA

CA

Babylonia and Sumeria

Mesopotamia is the Greek name for the lands of the Tigris and Euphrates rivers, currently occupied by Iraq and Syria. This region had no easily defensible frontiers, and throughout historical times fierce hill-people raided from the east, while herdsmen from the steppe overran the fertile lands from the west and south, as they saw the potential of cultivating its rich soil and fishing its rivers. The northern part of Mesopotamia has enough annual rainfall for farmers to grow grain and find pasture, and people have lived in its hills and near its rivers since Neolithic times, about 12,000 years ago.

In ancient Babylonia to the south, agriculture depended on artificial irrigation, drawing water from the rivers and carefully controlling it. This skill was apparently introduced there around 5000 BCE, after which settled life developed until the fourth millennium BCE, when great cities flourished by the rivers and canals. From these cities, traders and colonists spread north up the Euphrates river into Syria, east into Persia, and south down the Persian Gulf, carrying inventions and ideas from their culture – foremost among them writing. The need to organize and administer the large settlements and their irrigation systems stimulated the development of writing in Babylonia.

The Sumerians

The dominant people of the south, the Sumerians, produced Babylonian cuneiform writing – the most significant writing system of the ancient Middle East – on clay tablets. Their religious beliefs are the earliest we can know about in Mesopotamia, although it is impossible to be sure that any particular aspect is solely Sumerian because the land was always inhabited by a mixture of races. There is little that can be called distinctively 'Sumerian' apart from their language.

In Uruk (Erech), a city dating to c. 3000 BCE and best known from archaeological excavations and from the earliest texts, there were two main temples. One was for Anu, the supreme god, the king of heaven; the other for Inanna, the

great mother, goddess of fertility, love, and war. The goddess Inanna was the principle of life, depicted in paintings, carved into stone, and modelled in clay in almost every prehistoric dwelling.

The temples of Uruk employed large numbers of people and owned extensive estates. Craftsmen made fine artefacts for use in temple services, weavers made clothes for the sacred statues and for the priests, and scribes recorded temple affairs. The priests also played an important part in city life; the high priest was sometimes also king of the city. Such seems to have been the regular structure of temple life in Babylonian cities for centuries.

Each major city in the south was the centre for worship of a particular deity. During the third millennium BCE, besides Anu and Inanna at Uruk, there were: Enlil, lord of the atmosphere, who was worshipped at Nippur, and, next to Anu, chief of the gods; Enki, ruler of the fresh water from beneath the earth, who had his shrine at Eridu; the sun-god, Utu, whose home was at Larsa; and the moon-god, Nanna, who lived at Ur. Each principal god had a family and servants, who were also honoured with temples and chapels. For example, Enlil's son, Ninurta, was lord of Lagash. Lesser deities had shrines inside the larger temples, but were also revered in small shrines among the houses of the citizens.

The temples dominated the cities. When a temple grew old or was regarded as too small, a new one was built, often on the ruins of

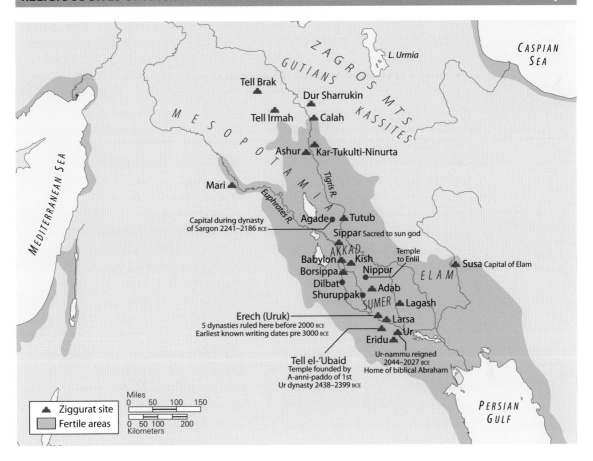

the previous one. Over the years, the temples came to be erected on platforms covering the earlier buildings, towering above the surrounding houses. Most important in these temples was the holy room, where the statue of the particular god stood. In Solomon's Temple, the Jewish sanctuary in Jerusalem, the holy room had no statue: solely the Ark of the Covenant.

'Ancient Egypt' is the civilization in the lower reaches of the Nile Valley from about 3100 BCE to 30 BCE. This includes periods of strength such as the Old Kingdom (c. 2700–2200 BCE), when a line of powerful rulers left their pyramids as monuments; the Middle Kingdom (c. 2000–1800 BCE), another time of strong central government, with influence on Egypt's neighbours; and the New Kingdom (c. 1550–1225 BCE), when Egypt was among the dominant countries of the Near East.

It also includes periods when Egypt was divided internally and occupied by foreign powers. These changes in political power and economic prosperity over 3,000 years occasioned changes in philosophical and religious attitudes; yet there are enough consistent features to allow us to talk about 'Egyptian religion'.

Egyptian gods

The gods of ancient Egypt – represented in the temples and tombs – are a bewildering mix of strange forms, half-animal and half-human. We know little about actual Egyptian religious beliefs, since we have no records about Egyptian theology by ancient Egyptians. Many of the Egyptian gods represented powerful natural forces. Egypt's prosperity depended on the daily reappearance of the sun and the annual flooding of the Nile: these forces were regarded as gods needing to be coaxed and encouraged through sacrifice and worship.

The gods were often originally linked with particular cities. As communities came together in larger political units, local deities gradually became important in the nation as a whole. For example, the god Amun, from the city of Thebes, was a kind of national god, protecting and leading the whole nation for a time during the New Kingdom, when Thebes was home to the ruling family. There

are also references to 'God' or 'The God', who seems to have been an unnamed universal divine power, controlling the universe and upholding good against evil.

For a short time, from about 1375 to 1350 BCE, there was an attempt to impose a form of monotheism. The pharaoh Amenophis IV gradually developed worship of the Aten, or the sun's disk, until he was the only god whose worship was tolerated. The worship of Amun was attacked, while the Aten was seen as the source of all life. This gift of life was passed to the king, who changed his name to Akhenaten – 'the one who is beneficial to the Aten' – and to his family, and thence to the people.

As well as the 'mainstream' gods, the Egyptians also adopted other deities. The king or pharaoh was also seen as a god, although this was a limited idea of divinity, because he was clearly mortal. Few rulers had a statue placed in the temple shrine as an object of worship. Animals also feature in Egyptian religion. In some instances, all the animals of one species were regarded as sacred, and were mummified and buried in huge numbers.

The Egyptians seem always to have believed in an afterlife. The earliest tombs contain items of food and equipment, and later the decoration of tombs shows how the Egyptians thought such a life would be: similar to this world – but better.

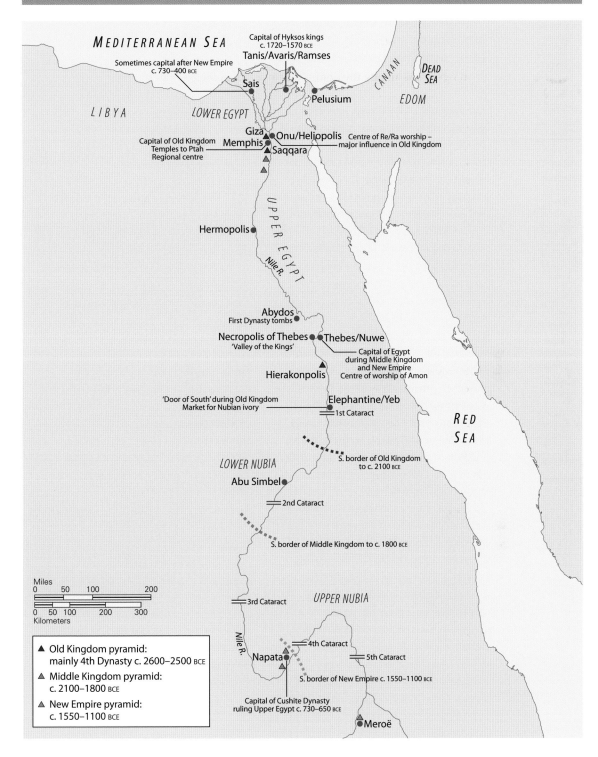

MEDITERRANEAN SEA

Capital of Hyksos kings
c. 1720–1570 BCE
Tanis/Avaris/Ramses

Sometimes capital after New Empire
c. 730–400 BCE

Sais

Pelusium

CANAAN

DEAD
SEA

EDOM

LIBYA

LOWER EGYPT

Giza
Capital of Old Kingdom
Temples to Ptah
Regional centre
Memphis
Onu/Heliopolis
Centre of Re/Ra worship –
major influence in Old Kingdom
Saqqara

UPPER EGYPT

Hermopolis

Nile R.

Abydos
First Dynasty tombs

Necropolis of Thebes
'Valley of the Kings'
Thebes/Nuwe
Capital of Egypt
during Middle Kingdom
and New Empire
Centre of worship of Amon
Hierakonpolis

'Door of South' during Old Kingdom
Market for Nubian ivory
Elephantine/Yeb
1st Cataract

RED
SEA

S. border of Old Kingdom
to c. 2100 BCE

LOWER NUBIA

Abu Simbel
2nd Cataract

S. border of Middle Kingdom to c. 1800 BCE

Miles
0 50 100   200

0 50 100   200   300
Kilometers

3rd Cataract

UPPER NUBIA

Nile R.

4th Cataract
Napata
5th Cataract

S. border of New Empire c. 1550–1100 BCE

Capital of Cushite Dynasty
ruling Upper Egypt c. 730–650 BCE

Meroë

▲ Old Kingdom pyramid:
mainly 4th Dynasty c. 2600–2500 BCE

▲ Middle Kingdom pyramid:
c. 2100–1800 BCE

▲ New Empire pyramid:
c. 1550–1100 BCE

The Early City Religions

The rise of city civilizations brought about important religious developments. Cities developed around 3500 BCE in Mesopotamia, and slightly later in Egypt. Urban civilization spread into the Indus Valley and rose independently in China.

The invention of the plough and introduction of irrigation greatly improved agricultural productivity, while the development of sea travel, rise of metallurgy, and invention of writing opened up for city-dwellers occupations other than farming. Increasing land and maritime contact with other societies facilitated the sharing of concepts, knowledge, and trade. Specialists uninvolved in agriculture – such as the Sumerian temple communities – now began to appear.

The rise of cities led to specialization: men began to adopt different trades and professions. Religion reflected this, with the arrival of distinct priesthoods, temples, festivals, theologies and, later, scriptures. Although the Neolithic inter-relationship between human beings, nature, and the gods continued, more personal religious questions – about suffering, meaning, and life after death – became more immediate. Religion was evolving into a separate, personal concern as well as a group affair.

Forms of urban religious life differed between Mesopotamia, Egypt, the Indus Valley and China. Religion in ancient Egypt was characterized by the worship of, and sacrifice to, local and state gods, in some instances in elaborate temples. In Mesopotamia there was a succession of peoples and religions, including the Sumerians, Babylonians, Assyrians, Hurrians, Hittites, and West Semitic groups. State religions, with their temples, kings, and annual festivals, were characterized by their mythologies: epic creation accounts, stories of ritual victories by god-kings such as Marduk,

ANCIENT EMPIRES OF THE MIDDLE EAST

Troy

Knossos

MEDITERRANEAN SEA

Miles
0   100   200

0   100   200   300
Kilometers

Memphis   Nile R.

and tales of myth-ritual state ceremonies. Out of this Egyptian and Middle Eastern setting, Jewish concerns for the land and ethical monotheism were later to emerge.

map 4

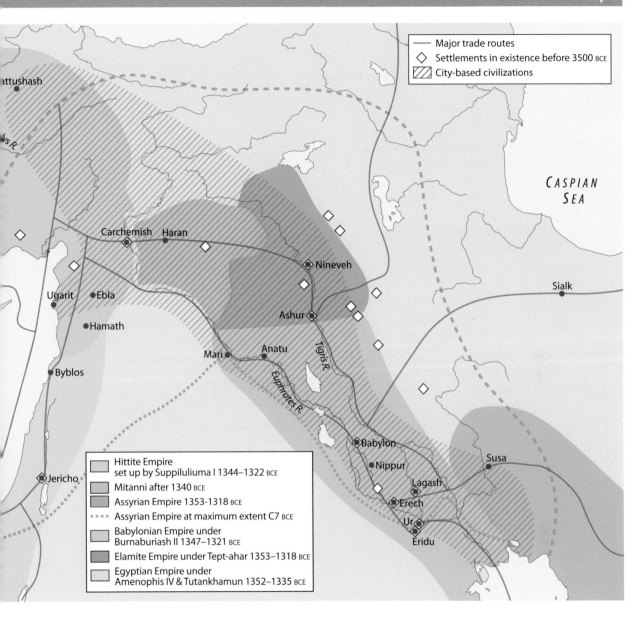

Hattushash

Carchemish   Haran

Ugarit   ● Ebla

● Hamath

● Byblos

◈ Jericho

Mari   Anatu

◈ Nineveh

◈ Ashur

Tigris R.

Euphrates R.

● Babylon
● Nippur

Lagash

◈ Erech

Ur ◈
Eridu

Susa

CASPIAN
SEA

● Sialk

Legend:
- —— Major trade routes
- ◇ Settlements in existence before 3500 BCE
- ▨ City-based civilizations

Hittite Empire
set up by Suppululiuma I 1344–1322 BCE

Mitanni after 1340 BCE

Assyrian Empire 1353-1318 BCE

••• Assyrian Empire at maximum extent C7 BCE

Babylonian Empire under
Burnaburiash II 1347–1321 BCE

Elamite Empire under Tept-ahar 1353–1318 BCE

Egyptian Empire under
Amenophis IV & Tutankhamun 1352–1335 BCE

THE EARLY CITY RELIGIONS   23

▲ Mt Erymanthus

DIONYSUS

Mt Pangaeus ▲

M A C E D O N I A

POSEIDON
THASOS

SAMOTHRACE
CABEIRI

HERMES

≡
Mt Olympus ▲
ZEUS, Olympian gods, muses

▲ *Mt Ossa*
PALLAS ATHENE

Tr●
LEMNOS   ▲ Mt Mosychlus

T H E S S A L Y

Ⅲ Dodona
ORACLE OF ZEUS

▲ *Mt Pelion*

LESBOS

A E G E A N
S E A

SKYROS

ASCLEPIOS

Mt Oeta ▲

M E D I T E R R A N E A N

S E A

≡
Mt Parnassus ▲
Pythian Games for Apollo ⦶● Delphi

LEBADAEA Ⅲ
Ⅲ Ⅲ

EUBOEA
POSEIDON, ARTEMIS

DIONYSOS
CHIOS

B O E T I A

Ⅲ AMPHIAREION OF OROPOS
▲● Cithaeron Mts

POSEIDON, APHRODITE
Isthmian Games
for Poseidon

Corinth
●⦶

▲ Mt Helicon

A C H A E A

Cyllene Mts ▲▲

Nemean Games
for Zeus

●● Nemea
● Mycenae

≡●Eleusis
Athens
⦶●

ANDROS

*PALLAS ATHENE,
ARTEMIS, DIONYSOS,
POSEIDON, HERMES*

DEMETER

A T T I C A

ICARIA

ARES

ZACYNTHUS

●⦶
Olympia

A R C A D I A

*PALLAS ATHENE
DIONYSOS*

Argos ●
HERA

●Epidaurus
ASCLEPIOS

Sunium ▲
POSEIDON

DELOS
APOLLO

NAXOS

PAROS

▲ *Mt Parthenius*

*APOLLO OF AMYCLAE,
ARTEMIS ORTHIA,
ATHENA CHALKIOIKOS,
DIOSCURI*

●Sparta
≡

L A C O N I A

MELOS

THERA

APHRODITE
CYTHERA

I O N I A N   S E A

APHRODITE
*from
Cyprus*

▲ Sacred mountain

≡ Cult site

⦶ Site of games/arts competition

Deity worshipped widely in area

Ⅲ Oracle

Miles
0   50   100

0   50   100   150
Kilometers

ZEUS

▲ Mt Ida

C R E T E

map 5

The Greeks and Romans created a world of gods and demi-gods, heroes, nymphs, and satyrs that linked heaven ('Olympia') and earth.

Well-known gods of antiquity were introduced, or taken over from previous or related sanctuaries and tribes: Poseidon (Roman Neptune), symbolic of the sea; Aphrodite (Roman Venus), symbolic of love; Ares (Roman Mars), of war; Hephaistos (Roman Vulcan), of fire. Zeus (Roman Jupiter), the god of thunder, became the father-god. Thus the Greeks created a myth that lent order and meaning to the complexities of life.

In early times, some of the gods were identified with, and worshipped in, particular places: Zeus in Crete; Hera in Argos; Apollo – the beardless youth, god variously of music, healing, sun, and light – in Asia Minor; and Dionysus (or Bacchus) – god of the grape harvest, wine, fertility, and ritual frenzy – in Mycenae. These gods gradually began to function more widely, and sometimes took on characteristics of other deities. For example the North African deities Baal and Tannit became respectively Saturn and the Heavenly Goddess (Roman *Dea Caelestis*); Apollo travelled from Didyma, Asia Minor to Delphi, Greece, and thence to Rome.

Mount Olympus became the meeting place of quasi-aristocratic gods, governed by Zeus and his jealous wife, Hera. Kronos (time) became the father of Zeus; Uranus (sky, or heaven) the father of Kronos – symbolically linking power, time, and heaven.

In *The Odyssey* and *The Iliad*, the ancient Greek poet Homer portrays the gods in human terms, although they are immortal. They prompt dread, fear, shame, and reverence in humans, who in response pray, praise, take oaths, sacrifice victims, and pour libations. The gods were consulted through

The Religions of Ancient Greece

The Tholos of Delphi, Greece, part of the Sanctuary of Athena Pronaia, built c. 370 BCE.

birds (augury) or interpretation of dreams. Other omens included lightning, thunder, and falling stars.

Greek religion dealt with some of the great metaphysical problems: fate (the Roman *Parcae)*, death (*Hades,* a place where life continued, with neither reward nor punishment), and good and evil. Some of the great mythic tales and characters came into being – such as Medea, Antigone, Oedipus, and Theseus – and were the subjects of dramatic works by major authors.

The ritual complex at Eleusis, West Attica, involved the goddess Demeter and her daughter and was linked to grain. At festival time participants in 'mystery' initiation were promised happiness and perhaps a vision of the god. The temple at Eleusis provided for huge gatherings of up to 10,000 people.

The Greek historian Herodotus (c. 484–425 BCE) claimed the most ancient oracle site in Greece was Dodona, with its great oak tree. Questions to this oracle reveal particular concerns about health. Other oracles were the Amphiareion of Oropos and Trophonius at Lebadaea.

The temple-cult of Asclepios, the god of healing, was established in times of need, especially by city-states threatened by disease. It became the most widespread of the newer cults, with important centres at Pergamum, Corinth, Epidaurus, and Kos. The cult used as remedies exercise, cold baths, rest, herbal prescriptions, and diet, along with dreams induced by suggestion.

Two syncretistic cults emerged from Egypt. The cult of Serapis fused the Greek mysteries with the native Egyptian cult of Osiris. In the cult of Isis – important in ancient myth as the king's divine mother – the king sat in Isis' lap, creating a 'madonna-and-child' image. Isis and Serapis were believed to be able to deliver from war, prison, pain, wandering, shipwreck, and even death.

Greek religion seems to have been more personal, individualistic, and pluralistic than the religion of the Romans, who emphasized the public, contractual aspects. Yet it is important not to impose a false dichotomy between the religion of these two civilizations.

Roman Religion

Roman religion was originally related to the agricultural economy. Rome's only unique mythology related to her own creation, with the city personified as the chief deity.

The Romans adopted many foreign gods – especially Greek – modifying them to fit their own needs. Three of the oldest deities – Jupiter, Juno, and Minerva (Greek Zeus, Hera, and Athena) – were worshipped in a temple on Rome's Capitoline Hill. Other later deities included Aesculapius (Greek Asclepios) from 293–291 BCE, and Cybele, the 'Great Mother', from 204 BCE. The Pantheon of Agrippa and Hadrian in Rome, commissioned during the reign of Augustus (r. 27 BCE–14 CE) and completed by Hadrian (r. 117–138 CE), was dedicated to the twelve planetary gods as an expression of cosmic order.

There does not seem to have been a priest class in Greece comparable to the priests (*pontifices*) of Rome. Augustus appropriated the ancient office of *pontifex maximus*, incorporating in his person the religious tradition of the city. Beginning with the Emperor Caligula (37 CE), the imperial oath included the name 'Augustus' between 'Zeus the Saviour' and 'the holy Virgin of our city'. This concept of emperor worship can be traced back to Hellenistic, Oriental, and pre-Roman Western models of deified kingship.

Evidence from the excavated city of Pompeii, Italy, shows that family cults flourished. Almost every house and workshop had a private shrine with busts of ancestors and other traditional household gods, the Lares and Penates. The preserved ruins of Ostia include by the 3rd century CE fifteen shrines devoted to the god Mithras, whose mystery cult flourished from the 1st to the 4th century CE.

SOURCES OF THE ROMAN CULTS

map 6

Roman Empire circa CE 117
Source of Roman cult/belief system

GERMANIA

Lauriacum

guntum

diolanum
(Milan)

Aquileia

Danube R.

Salonae

ITALIA

Rome

BLACK SEA

Sinope

Philippi

THRACE

Byzantium

Thessalonica

Orphic Rites

Cabiri

SAMOTHRACE

Troas

Orphic Rites

Pergamum

PHRYGIA

PERSIA

LESBOS

Dionysus

ACHAIA

Thebes

Smyrna

Delphi

Ephesus

Corinth

Athens

Miletus

Mithras

Edessa

Hierapolis

Syracuse

Apollo

ales

Poseidon

RHODES

Antioch

Salamis

PHOENICIA

Palmyra

arthage

MEDITERRANEAN

Pallas Athene

CRETE

CYPRUS

Aphrodite

Dionysus

Gortyna

Adonis

Rhea

Adonis

Byblos

Helios

Damascus

SEA

Leptis Magna

Cyrene

Isis, Osiris, Serapis

Caesarea

Jerusalem

LIBYA

Alexandria

Memphis

ARABIA

EGYPT

A

Nile R.

RED
SEA

Zoroastrianism

Zoroaster is the westernized version of 'Zarathushtra', the prophet of ancient Persia, who may have lived c. 1200 BCE, when Persia was emerging from the Stone Age. From the age of 30, Zoroaster had a series of visions that inspired him to preach a new message, which became the recognized teaching of a small kingdom in north-east Persia. In time it spread throughout Persia, where it became the official religion for 1,000 years.

Zoroastrians believe their prophet was chosen by God to receive his unique revelation, contained in 17 hymns, the *Gathas*, central to a major act of worship, *yasna*. Zarathushtra emphasized personal religion: all men and women have a personal responsibility to choose between good and evil, and will be judged hereafter. He taught that God – Ahura Mazda, the Wise Lord – was the wholly good creator of all things and is friend of all. Evil in the world comes from Angra Mainyu, the destructive spirit, who created demons, rules in hell, and from the beginning opposed God. The world is a battleground between the forces of good and evil: humankind was created to aid God in this conflict.

God also created a number of heavenly beings, foremost among them Amesha Spentas, the 'Bounteous Immortals', or sons and daughters of God: Vohu Manah, good mind; Asha, righteousness; Armaiti, devotion; Kshathra, dominion; Haurvatat, wholeness; and Ameretat, immortality. These are both heavenly beings and ideals to which the righteous should aspire.

Zarathushtra taught that the world was essentially good, but spoilt by the attacks of evil. He looked toward a day when the battle with evil would climax, the good triumph, and the world be restored to its perfect state. At the last, the dead will be raised and judged, the wicked will go to hell, and the righteous live with God in perfection for eternity.

We have no written sources for Zoroastrianism's first 700 years. By the time the Persians came to power in the 6th century BCE, the religion was already widespread. The Achaemenid dynasty that ruled Persia after Cyrus the Great (d. 530 BCE) spread Zoroastrianism throughout the realm, largely through a priestly tribe of Medes called 'Magi'. During the ensuing Parthian Empire (247 BCE–224 CE), steps were taken to collect the ancient traditions and sacred literature in the Zoroastrian holy book, the Avesta.

From earliest times, fire has been the focus of Zoroastrian rites and devotions. Temples were introduced into the religion by the Achaemenid monarch, Artaxerxes II (404–359 BCE). At the centre of their sacred buildings Zoroastrians placed the 'icon' of fire.

When the Islamic empire rose to power, education, promotion, and equality before the law were denied to Zoroastrians, who were forced to retreat to desert villages. Oppressed and poor, they were frequently attacked by Muslims. For almost 1,400 years of Muslim rule, Zoroastrians endured persecution, oppression, poverty, injustice, and isolation.

In the 10th century CE, a small group of Zoroastrians left Persia to seek religious freedom, settling in India, where they have since lived in peace and security. Today Parsis and Iranian Zoroastrians are reckoned to number between 124,000 and 190,000 worldwide, with the main base of their religion in India.

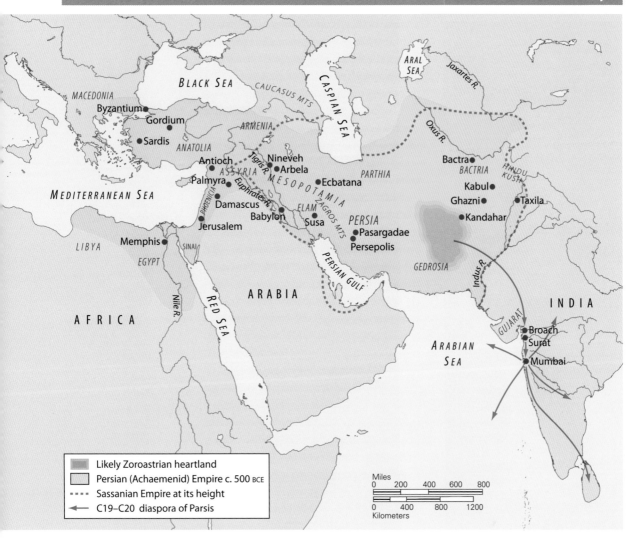

MACEDONIA
Byzantium
Gordium
Sardis
ANATOLIA
BLACK SEA
CAUCASUS MTS
CASPIAN SEA
ARAL SEA
Jaxartes R.
ARMENIA
Oxus R.
Antioch
ASSYRIA
Nineveh
Arbela
PARTHIA
Bactra
BACTRIA
HINDU KUSH
Palmyra
Tigris R.
MESOPOTAMIA
Ecbatana
Kabul
Euphrates R.
PHOENICIA
Damascus
ELAM
Ghazni
Taxila
Babylon
Susa
PERSIA
Kandahar
Jerusalem
ZAGROS MTS
Pasargadae
Persepolis
MEDITERRANEAN SEA
Memphis
SINAI
LIBYA
EGYPT
PERSIAN GULF
GEDROSIA
Indus R.
INDIA
AFRICA
Nile R.
RED SEA
ARABIA
GUJARAT
Broach
Surat
Mumbai
ARABIAN SEA

Legend:
- Likely Zoroastrian heartland
- Persian (Achaemenid) Empire c. 500 BCE
- - - - Sassanian Empire at its height
- ⟵ C19–C20 diaspora of Parsis

Miles
0   200   400   600   800
0   400   800   1200
Kilometers

Part 2

Hinduism

The Origins of Hinduism

The religion we know today as Hinduism may be almost as old as Indian civilization itself. Archaeological evidence suggests continuities between the religion of the Indus Valley society of 2500–1500 BCE and modern Hinduism.

Archaeological excavations have revealed evidence of what appears to be a highly developed urban culture – sometimes also known as the 'Harappa Culture' – with well-developed systems of farming, grain-storage, and pottery. However little is known about the religion of this civilization. The large number of terracotta figurines unearthed suggests continuity with later Hindu deities, such as Shiva and the mother goddess, but scholars are wary of making definitive connections. The Indus Valley civilization seems to have declined suddenly between 1800 and 1700 BCE.

What followed is the subject of academic controversy. Some scholars claim the Indus Valley civilization was replaced by the culture of the Aryans, Indo-European invaders, or migrants from the Caucasus region, who moved south and settled in the Indian subcontinent. However others believe this Aryan civilization developed from within the Indus Valley, or Harappa, culture.

An Iron Age culture, known by the style of its pottery, as The Painted Grey Ware culture, flourished from 1000 to 500 BCE, and was succeeded by the Northern Black Polished Ware culture from about 500 BCE. Whatever its origins, the history of Hinduism is the story of the next 2,000 years of Aryan culture, often interacting with, and always dominating, non-Aryan cultures in the area.

The language of the Aryans was Sanskrit, and our knowledge of the early Aryans derives mainly from ancient Sanskrit compositions – the Vedas – compiled over centuries, and originating in oral traditions from thousands of years earlier. The religion of this period is variously known as Vedism, ancient Hinduism, Brahmanism, and Vedic Brahmanism. Many Hindus regard the Vedas as a timeless revelation, the repository of all knowledge, and a marker of Hindu identity: the Vedas form the foundation for most of the later developments in Hinduism. The earliest Vedas were mainly liturgical texts, used primarily in rituals of sacrifice addressed to such early gods as Agni, the fire god, and Soma, the plant god.

In due course, Aryan culture became well established in northern India. Brahmanic (or Vedic) ideology, central to social and political life, was concerned with the ritual status and duties of the king, the maintenance of social order, and the regulation of individual behaviour in accordance with the all-embracing ideology of duty or righteousness (*dharma*). Dharma involved ritual and moral behaviour, and defined good conduct according to such factors as class (*varna*) and stage in life (*ashrama*). It operated simultaneously at several levels: the transcendental and eternal (*sanatana dharma*), the everyday (*sadharana dharma*), and the individual and personal (*svadharma*). Neglecting *dharma* was believed to lead to undesirable social and personal consequences.

The later Vedic Period

In later Vedic texts – the Aranyakas and Upanishads – ritual practice began to be seen as secondary to the gaining of spiritual knowledge. Central to this was the *karma-samsara-moksha* doctrine: all beings are reincarnated into the world (*samsara*) over and over again; the results of action (*karma*) are reaped in future lives. This process of endless rebirth is characterized by suffering (*dukkha*); liberation (*moksha*) from

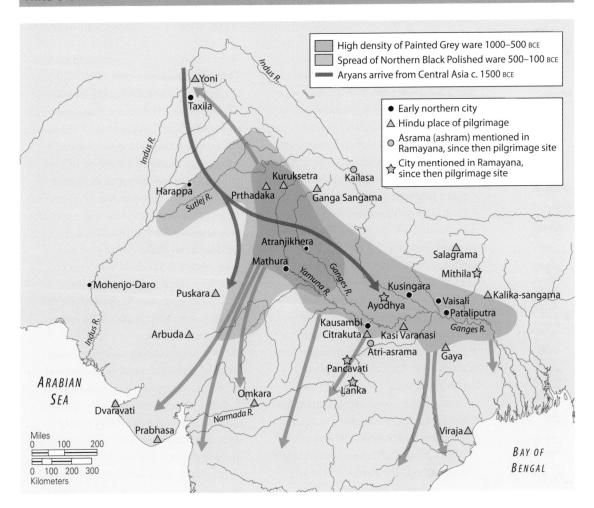

High density of Painted Grey ware 1000–500 BCE
Spread of Northern Black Polished ware 500–100 BCE
Aryans arrive from Central Asia c. 1500 BCE

● Early northern city
△ Hindu place of pilgrimage
◉ Asrama (ashram) mentioned in Ramayana, since then pilgrimage site
☆ City mentioned in Ramayana, since then pilgrimage site

this suffering can be obtained by gaining spiritual knowledge.

Gaining spiritual knowledge thus came to assume central importance, and the self-discipline and ascetic methods necessary to gain it were developed in the Hindu traditions of yoga and renunciation of the world. Ascetic groups known as strivers (*sramanas*) were formed during this period, seeking liberation through austerity. Buddhism and Jainism – both of which rejected the authority of the Vedas – originated in these groups.

Hindu Temple Worship

Sectarian worship of particular deities grew and flourished in India through much of the first millennium CE. Increasingly, Vedic sacrifice was marginalized, giving way to devotional worship, or *puja* – the ritual expression of love or devotion (*bhakti*) to a deity.

Sanskrit narrative traditions also grew and flourished, most important of which were the Hindu epics – the *Ramayana* and the *Mahabharata* (the Puranas), devotional texts containing mythological stories about the gods and goddesses and treatises on ritual worship – and devotional poetry in Indian regional languages, particularly Tamil. One of the most important developments of this period was the composition of the *Bhagavad Gita*, the 'Song of the Lord', contained in the *Mahabharata*. This work, perhaps the most famous of the Hindu scriptures, expresses in narrative form the concerns of Hinduism: the importance of *dharma* and the maintenance of social order and stability, together with the importance of devotion to the transcendent as a personal god.

Temple cities grew and flourished during this period, serving not only as commercial and administrative cores of kingdoms, but as ritual centres. The temple was normally located at the heart of the town, and thus of the kingdom. Kings sought to derive legitimacy through their patronage of these ritual sites, dedicated to one or the other of the major deities of the Purana.

Temple cults

In early medieval India the worship of Vishnu or one of his incarnations – normally Krishna or Rama (Vaisnavism) – and worship of Shiva (Shaivism or Saivam) became widespread throughout the subcontinent, promoting temple-cults and displacing Buddhism. Sectarian devotional groups emerged, dedicated to the worship of Vishnu (Vaishnavas), Shiva (Shaivas), and the goddess Devi (Shaktas).

From medieval times, many temples – known as 'Sakta' temples – were also devoted to goddesses. Such temples still dot the countryside, a distinctive feature of modern Hinduism.

Within each temple stood a consecrated icon, regarded as a partial embodiment of the deity. Manuals known as *Agamas*, *Tantras*, and *Sarnhitas* described the rituals to be performed during temple worship. In the temple, a daily ritual known as *puja* involved waking, dressing, bathing, feeding, and entertaining the god, as though he were a king. Such static images of the deity were hidden in a holy place inside the temple, but often had movable equivalents that were processed through the village or city on festival days.

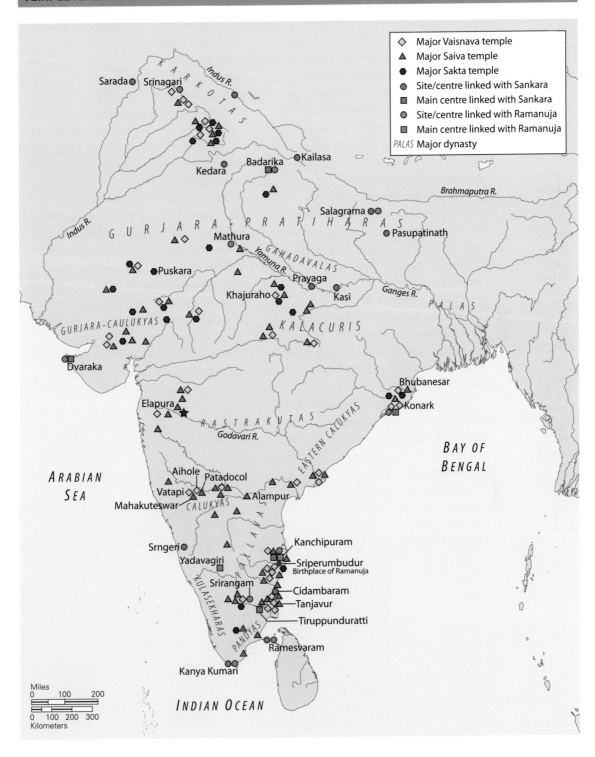

Major Vaisnava temple
Major Saiva temple
Major Sakta temple
Site/centre linked with Sankara
Main centre linked with Sankara
Site/centre linked with Ramanuja
Main centre linked with Ramanuja
PALAS Major dynasty

Sarada
Srinagari
KARKOTAS
Indus R.

Kailasa
Badarika
Kedara

Brahmaputra R.

Salagrama
Pasupatinath

Indus R.
GURJARA - PRATIHARAS

Mathura
GAHADAVALAS
Yamuna R.

Puskara
Prayaga
Khajuraho
Kasi
Ganges R.
PALAS

GURJARA-CAULUKYAS
KALACURIS

Dvaraka

Bhubanesar
Elapura
Konark

RASTRAKUTAS
Godavari R.
EASTERN CALUKYAS

BAY OF
BENGAL

ARABIAN
SEA

Aihole
Patadocol
Vatapi
Alampur
Mahakuteswar
CALUKYAS

PALLAVAS

Srngeri
Kanchipuram
Yadavagiri
Sriperumbudur
Birthplace of Ramanuja
Srirangam
Cidambaram
KULASEKHARAS
Tanjavur
Tiruppunduratti

Ramesvaram
PANDYAS
Kanya Kumari

Miles
0   100   200

0 100 200 300
Kilometers

INDIAN OCEAN

Hinduism and the Sacred

By tradition there are seven sites of particular religious significance for Hindus. These are Varanasi, associated with Shiva; Kanchipuram, the site of a temple devoted to Shiva; Haridwar; Ujjain; Ayodhya; and Mathura and Dwarka, both linked to Krishna. The land of India itself is worshipped as 'Divine Mother' (*Bharat Mata*) and is sanctified by *Shaktipithas*, centres of goddess worship.

Particularly important to Hinduism are sacred rivers, and the holy towns and cities situated along their banks, which are seen as crossing-places (*tirtha*) between the secular and the sacred, and between the world of the living and the dead.

Hinduism lists seven sacred rivers: the Ganges, Saraswati (a legendary watercourse whose whereabouts is disputed), Yamuna, Indus, Narmada, Godavari, and Kaveri (Cauvery). Of these, the Ganges (*Ganga*), said to have come down from the stars, is the most important. Thousands take a daily dip in its waters, fulfilling the ritual purification that is vital in Hinduism. A single immersion in the river is believed to earn great spiritual merit for the worshipper. Known as the 'Great Mother', the Ganges has today become heavily polluted. In a single five-mile stretch of the 1,560 mile-long river, some 60,000 people ritually cleanse themselves every day. Yet parts of the river are so polluted by untreated sewage, industrial waste, and pesticides that they are not just filthy but disease-carrying, toxic, and carcinogenic. Hundreds of millions of dollars have been spent in attempts to cleanse the river, but with little success. Part of the problem is that the Ganges is regarded by Hindus as so sacred as to be beyond harm. Its waters are believed to be pure – even medicinal – and the responsibility of the gods, not of humans.

In Hinduism, the sacred is everywhere, not merely in temples and sacred images, but also in nature – in stones, trees, mountains, and rivers. From time to time the sacred reveals itself in the form of an arcane rock, stream, or spring, and the site of such a manifestation becomes a place of worship. Pilgrims flock to these places during auspicious months in the Hindu calendar, and mythological stories spring up concerning the miraculous nature of the pilgrimage site.

Indian sadhu near the Ganges river at Haridwar, Uttarakhand, India.

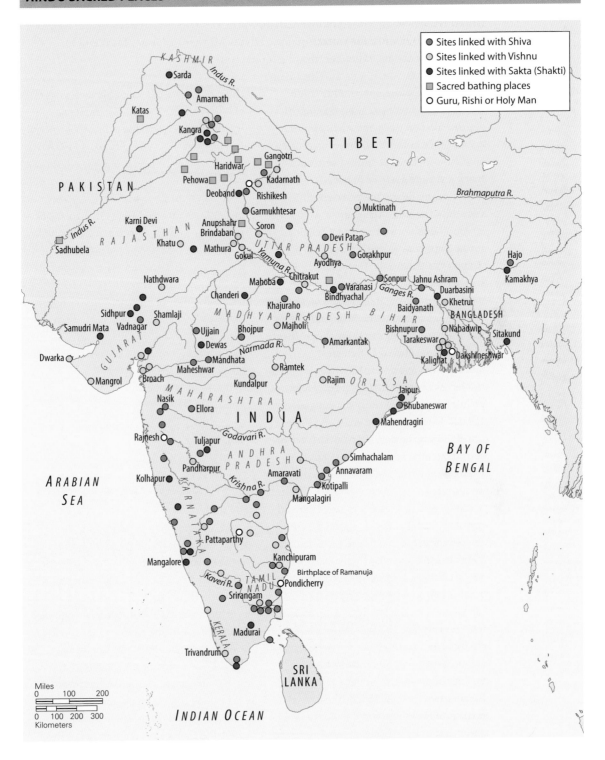

Legend:
- Sites linked with Shiva
- Sites linked with Vishnu
- Sites linked with Sakta (Shakti)
- Sacred bathing places
- Guru, Rishi or Holy Man

KASHMIR

Indus R.

Sarda

Amarnath

Katas

Kangra

TIBET

Brahmaputra R.

PAKISTAN

Gangotri

Haridwar

Kadarnath

Pehowa

Deoband

Rishikesh

Muktinath

Karni Devi

Garmukhtesar

Anupshahr

Brindaban

Soron

Devi Patan

Indus R.

RAJASTHAN

Khatu

Sadhubela

Mathura

Gokul

Yamuna R.

Gorakhpur

Hajo

Ayodhya

Kamakhya

Nathdwara

Mahoba

Chitrakut

Sonpur

Jahnu Ashram

Chanderi

Khajuraho

Varanasi

Ganges R.

Duarbasini

Baidyanath

Khetrur

Sidhpur

Shamlaji

MADHYA PRADESH

Bindhyachal

BIHAR

BANGLADESH

Samudri Mata

Vadnagar

Ujjain

Bhojpur

Majholi

Bishnupur

Nabadwip

Sitakund

GUJARAT

Dewas

Amarkantak

Tarakeswar

Dwarka

Narmada R.

Mandhata

Ramtek

Kalighat

Dakshineshwar

Mangrol

Broach

Maheshwar

Kundalpur

Rajim

ORISSA

MAHARASHTRA

Nasik

Ellora

INDIA

Jaipur

Bhubaneswar

Rajnesh

Tuljapur

Godavari R.

Mahendragiri

Pandharpur

ANDHRA PRADESH

Simhachalam

Kolhapur

Amaravati

Annavaram

BAY OF BENGAL

Krishna R.

Kotipalli

ARABIAN SEA

Mangalagiri

KARNATAKA

Pattaparthy

Mangalore

Kanchipuram

Birthplace of Ramanuja

Kaveri R.

TAMIL NADU

Pondicherry

Srirangam

KERALA

Madurai

Trivandrum

SRI LANKA

Miles
0   100   200

0 100 200 300
Kilometers

INDIAN OCEAN

Hinduism has been regarded as a 'world religion' since only the 19th century. Hindu reformers and Western orientalists then began to refer to the variety of beliefs and practices characterizing religious life in South Asia as 'Hinduism'.

Yet Hinduism possesses many features characteristic of 'indigenous religions'. It has no single historical founder, no central revelation, no creed or unified system of belief, no single doctrine of salvation, and no centralized authority. In this way, it differs from the other world religions.

Huge diversity and variety of religious movements, systems, beliefs, and practices characterize Hinduism. There is no clear division between the sacred and profane, the natural and supernatural: religion and social life are inseparable. Yet most scholars agree that unifying strands run through the diverse traditions constituting Hinduism.

Hinduism has seen many changes during its long history: for instance the rise and fall in prominence of some ancient gods, such as Indra, king of the gods, and Varuna, god of the sea; the decline in importance of the fire sacrifice; and the rise in popularity of the *bhakti* devotional tradition in the 6th century CE.

Influenced by Western values, 19th and early 20th century Hindu reformers such as Vivekananda (1863–1902), Ram Mohan Roy (1772–1833), Mohandas (Mahatma) Gandhi (1869–1948), and Sarvepalli Radhakrishnan (1888–1975) advocated an ethical form of Hinduism that campaigned against social practices such as *sati* – the self-immolation of widows on their husbands' funeral pyres – and child marriage. Hinduism has since retreated somewhat from these reforms, though *sati* is rare and strictly proscribed in India. Some Hindus today uphold traditional Hindu practices, and consult astrologers and

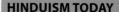

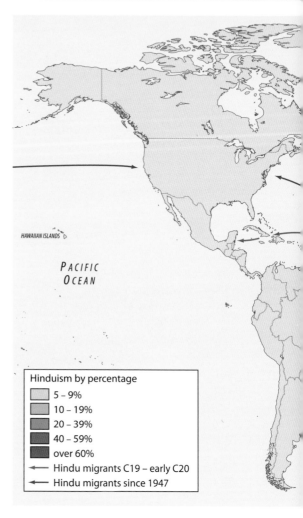

Hinduism by percentage
- 5 – 9%
- 10 – 19%
- 20 – 39%
- 40 – 59%
- over 60%
- ← Hindu migrants C19 – early C20
- ← Hindu migrants since 1947

gurus. Since Indian independence, Hinduism has also become more politicized, with the rise of Hindu nationalistic parties promoting India as a Hindu state.

Hinduism has also transcended national boundaries. While it has long flourished beyond the Indian subcontinent, in such places as Java and Bali, in the 20th century the Hindu diaspora became widespread, establishing communities across the globe.

Many Hindus migrated to the West, where their minority communities evolved

map 11

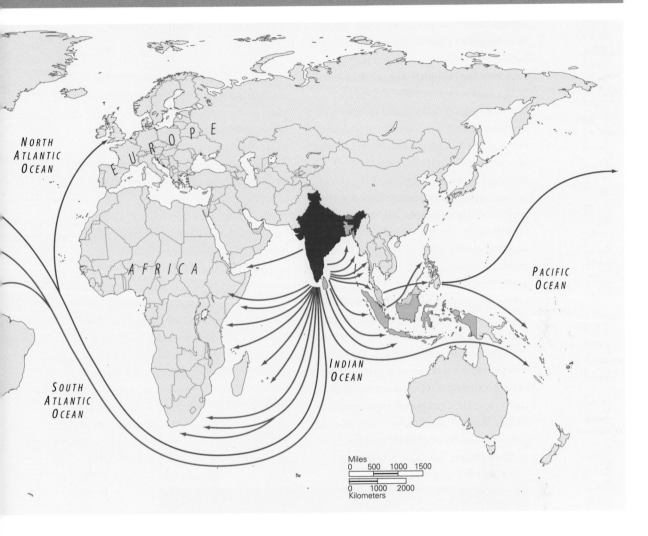

a distinctive form of Hinduism. Westernized Hindu ideas were imported back to India, increasing awareness of mystical traditions, sacred sites, and esoteric forms of spirituality. Interest has grown in pilgrimage to sacred shrines, such as the Sabarimala temple in Kerala, and in festivals such as the Kumbh Mela.

Modern Hinduism has also seen a strengthening of the caste system. At the turn of the 20th century, Hindu reformers sought to reform what they saw as the chauvinism and discrimination of the caste system. Revisionist thinking now emphasizes the positive side of castes. At the same time, some 'untouchable' and tribal groups have begun to abandon their traditional deities and practices to build temples and worship Hindu deities such as Vishnu and Shiva.

Apart from Hindu fundamentalism, Hinduism seems at ease with the modern world. Yoga and the related spiritual disciplines have been widely adopted and Hindu spiritual teachers are active worldwide.

Jainism – like Hinduism and Buddhism – emerged from the Vedic culture of northern India in about the 5th century BCE and is based around the teachings of Mahavira, whom Jains venerate as the 24th *jina* ('conquerer') of the last cosmic cycle. Jain tradition dates Mahavira to 599–527 BCE.

Jains hold that all living beings have a soul, and that these souls – undergoing a continuous cycle of death and rebirth – can be liberated only if the individual adopts an extreme ascetic lifestyle in order to become omniscient, following the example of Mahavira himself.

In the years after Mahavira's death, Jains broke into two main sects, Digambara and Shvetambara, which are divided by their views on scripture. Shvetambara Jains believe that their canon descends directly from *The Twelve-limbed Basket*, the collection of Mahavira's teachings, while Digambara Jains believe this has been lost. They also differ over whether there have been female *jinas*.

Monasticism is important in Jainism because of the value placed on asceticism. The co-dependence of ascetics and the laity is central to the structure of traditional Jain society. Because they believe all living beings have souls, Jains are bound by a strict code of ethics centred on the principle of non-violence, which forbids causing harm to *any* creature. Jains often have to compromise on some of their stricter ethical rules in order to live in the modern world. For instance although some ascetic Jains refuse to use electrical equipment, believing it may harm tiny creatures, most accept scientific and technological discoveries.

In the centuries after Mahavira's death, Jainism spread throughout India, which remains its primary home. Diaspora communities do exist, though these are small and restricted by the absence of ascetics, who are allowed to travel only on foot. There are more than three million Jains in the world, the majority in India. Digambara Jains live predominantly in the Deccan, Delhi, East Rajasthan, and neighbouring Madhya Pradesh; Shvetambara Jains live predominantly in Mumbai, Delhi, Rajasthan, Gujarat, and Madhya Pradesh. There are also Jain communities in East Africa, Europe, and North America.

Part of the ornately carved ceiling of the ancient Jain Sun Temple, Ranakpur, Rajasthan, India.

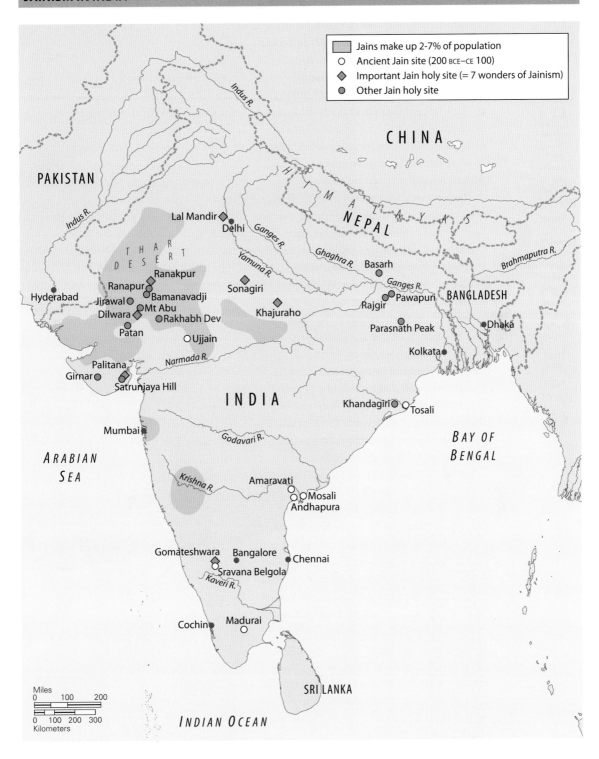

Jains make up 2-7% of population
○ Ancient Jain site (200 BCE–CE 100)
◇ Important Jain holy site (= 7 wonders of Jainism)
● Other Jain holy site

CHINA

PAKISTAN

Indus R.

Indus R.

H I M A L A Y A S

NEPAL

Ganges R.

Yamuna R.

Ghaghra R.

Brahmaputra R.

THAR DESERT

Lal Mandir ◇ ● Delhi

Basarh ●

Ganges R.

Ranakpur ◇

Ranapur ●

Bamanavadji ●

Sonagiri ◇

Rajgir ● Pawapuri ●

BANGLADESH

Hyderabad ●

Jirawal ●
Dilwara ● Mt Abu ◇
● Rakhabh Dev
Patan ●

Khajuraho ◇

Parasnath Peak ●

Dhaka ●

○ Ujjain

Kolkata ●

Palitana ◇
Girnar ●
Satrunjaya Hill ◇

Narmada R.

I N D I A

Khandagiri ● ○ Tosali

BAY OF BENGAL

Mumbai ●

Godavari R.

ARABIAN SEA

Krishna R.

Amaravati ○
○ Mosali
Andhapura ○

Gomateshwara ◇ Bangalore ●
○ Sravana Belgola

Chennai ●

Kaveri R.

Cochin ○ Madurai ●

SRI LANKA

Miles
0   100   200

0 100 200 300
Kilometers

INDIAN OCEAN

Part 3

Buddhism

The Origins of Buddhism

'Buddhism' is an English name for a religion often called by its adherents the *Dharma*, meaning both 'the teaching' and 'the way things are'. It is named after the Buddha, 'the one who has awakened'.

The traditional date for the birth of Buddha, who lived in north India for 80 years, is 563 BCE. However most historians today place him about a century later and his death around 400 BCE. The Buddha's clan-name was Gautama, but later tradition called him Siddhartha.

Buddhists tend to emphasize not Buddha but his teaching, which – they say – leads people to understand how things truly are, and then radically to reassess their lives. The Buddha awakened to this truth and taught it.

Who was the Buddha?

Buddhism has always been more interested in how the Buddha's life story illustrates Buddhist teachings than in its historical truth. The legendary account of his life – a prince who was protected from any knowledge of the unpleasant aspects of life – developed in the centuries after his death. According to alternative Pali language sources, the Buddha was a high-born Shakyan who was protected from awareness of suffering as he grew up, but the shock of encountering old age, sickness, and death led to his renouncing worldly pursuits. He was already married with a son, but now left his family and took up the life of a wandering seeker. He sought the truth that would lead to complete freedom from suffering – a life of meditation, study, and asceticism – and obtained food by asking for alms.

Eventually, through deep meditation, Siddhartha came to 'see it the way it really is' and this truth set him free. He was now the awakened one, the 'Buddha'. He gathered around him a group of disciples and wandered northern India, teaching all who would listen. The Buddha died in old age, though for him death was nothing.

What did he teach?

The Buddha taught that 'seeing things the way they really are' is the way to overcome every sort of unpleasantness, imperfection, and frustration – *dukkha*, literally 'pain' or 'suffering'. He taught that, when we look deeply, we can see our lives are at root simply *dukkha*.

In the Buddhist tradition a creator-God does not exist. Suffering is the result of our ignorance – not understanding the way things really are. Central to this misunderstanding is failure to appreciate that everything is by nature impermanent. We need to learn to let go of attachments and a deep-rooted fixed sense of selfhood, since we have been confused and suffered for infinite lifetimes.

At death the body ceases, but the ever-flowing continuum of consciousness and its mental accompaniments continues and 'spins' another body according to our good or bad deeds (*karma*). Such 'rebirth' means that we are yet again subject to suffering – old age, sickness, and death. This process ceases only with letting go at the deepest level, attained through meditation – a cessation Buddhists call 'enlightenment' (in Sanskrit, '*nirvana*').

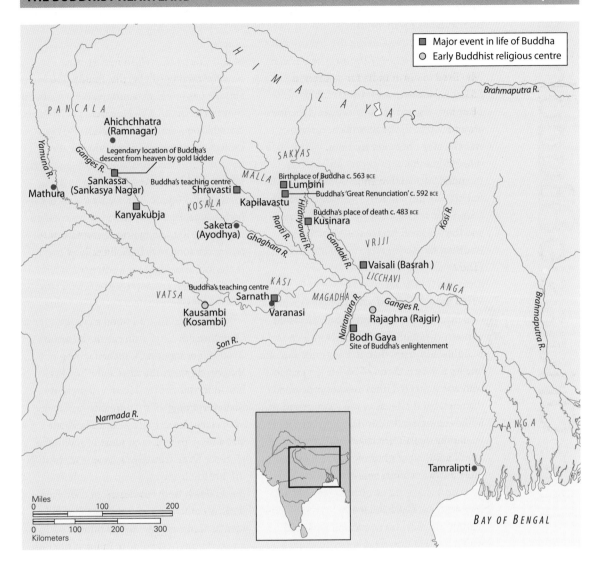

Major event in life of Buddha

Early Buddhist religious centre

Brahmaputra R.

H I M A L A Y 8 A S

Yamuna R.

P A N C A L A

Ahichchhatra
(Ramnagar)

SAKYAS

Ganges R.

MALLA

Birthplace of Buddha c. 563 BCE

Legendary location of Buddha's
descent from heaven by gold ladder

Buddha's teaching centre

Sankassa
(Sankasya Nagar)

Shravasti

Lumbini

Mathura

KOSALA

Kapilavastu

Buddha's 'Great Renunciation' c. 592 BCE

Kanyakubja

Hiranyavati R.

Buddha's place of death c. 483 BCE

Kusinara

Saketa
(Ayodhya)

Rapti R.

Ghaghara R.

Gandaki R.

VRJJI

Kosi R.

Vaisali (Basrah)

LICCHAVI

ANGA

KASI

VATSA

Buddha's teaching centre

Sarnath

MAGADHA

Nairanjara R.

Ganges R.

Brahmaputra R.

Kausambi
(Kosambi)

Varanasi

Rajaghra (Rajgir)

Bodh Gaya
Site of Buddha's enlightenment

Son R.

Narmada R.

V A N G A

Tamralipti

Miles
0   100   200

0   100   200   300
Kilometers

BAY OF BENGAL

What is Buddhism?

Central to the Buddha's vision of the way ahead was an order of monks and nuns – known as the *Sangha* – living on alms and expressing their commitment to radical transformation by renunciation. In time monasteries were established, together with a monastic rule regulating the conduct of the *Sangha*.

The Buddha did not appoint a successor, reportedly declaring that the teaching – the *Dharma* – should be his successor. However after his death disagreements occurred, initially over the monastic rules. Where such disputes could not be reconciled, monks in the minority had to leave, resulting in the formation of a number of different monastic traditions. The best known of these – the only early Indian Buddhist monastic tradition extant – is the 'Way of the Elders' (Theravada), found today in Sri Lanka, Thailand, Cambodia, and Myanmar (Burma).

In time different doctrinal positions also evolved, sometimes followed by identifiable schools. For example, the school known as Pudgalavada urged that, although the Buddha taught 'not-self', there still exists the *pudgala*, something 'in' us. Other debates concerned who or what the Buddha was. Some claimed a Buddha is more extraordinary than people realize: he doesn't *need* to sleep, defecate, or even eat, but does so merely to meet human expectations.

Mahayana Buddhism

The most significant development within Buddhism, the growth of the Mahayana – the 'Great Vehicle' – appeared in texts from around the 1st century CE. Mahayana Buddhism is not a doctrinal school or monastic tradition, and it makes no sense to speak of two 'schools' of Buddhism, Theravada and Mahayana. Mahayana is essentially a vision of what Buddhism is *really* all about.

Mahayana appears first in the Mahayana sutras, which claim – controversially – to be the words of the Buddha himself. These writings distinguish between being free from all suffering – 'enlightened' – and being a Buddha. A Buddha is more than just liberated from his own suffering; a Buddha is also perfectly compassionate. A Buddha also possesses miraculous abilities to help others. It takes many lifetimes of spiritual striving to become a Buddha. Those who aim for the highest goal seek not just their own freedom from suffering and rebirth, but also vow to follow the long path to Buddhahood over numerous rebirths.

The Mahayana is the way of those who aspire to become perfect Buddhas. Those who vow to do so are known as *bodhisattvas*. Over time, the Mahayana elaborated how a Buddha is superior to someone who has simply put an end to their suffering. Even his death was put on in order to present a 'skilful teaching' of impermanence. For the Mahayana, the Buddha – indeed infinite Buddhas – are still around, living on higher planes – 'Pure Lands' – from which, through their compassion and with miraculous powers, they help those in need. With them are advanced *bodhisattvas*, also full of compassion and able to help others.

Particularly significant in the history of Buddhism in India was the conversion of the great Emperor Ashoka (3rd century BCE), which gave the religion important imperial patronage – although scholars now reject the view that he attempted to make Buddhism the state religion.

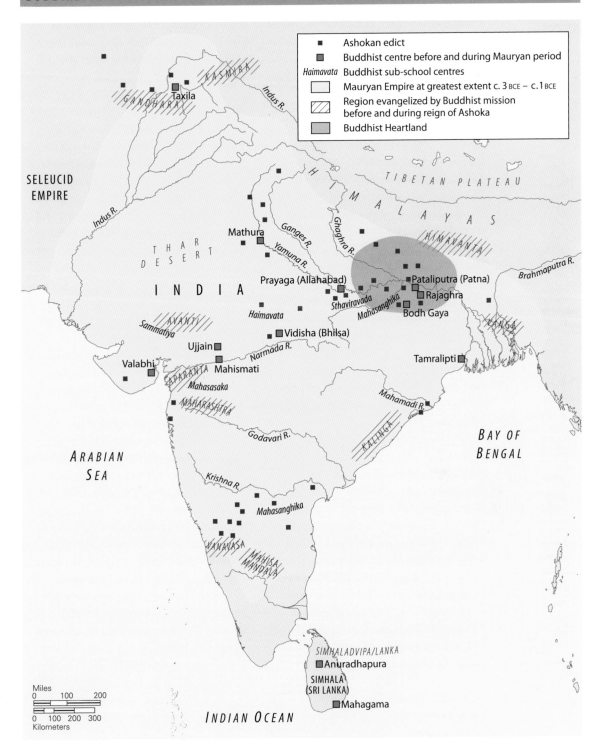

Ashokan edict

Buddhist centre before and during Mauryan period

Haimavata Buddhist sub-school centres

Mauryan Empire at greatest extent c. 3 BCE – c. 1 BCE

Region evangelized by Buddhist mission before and during reign of Ashoka

Buddhist Heartland

SELEUCID EMPIRE

KASMIRA

GANDHARA

Taxila

Indus R.

Indus R.

TIBETAN PLATEAU

H I M A L A Y A S

HIMANANTA

Brahmaputra R.

THAR DESERT

I N D I A

Mathura

Ganges R.

Yamuna R.

Ghaghra R.

Prayaga (Allahabad)

Haimavata

Sthaviravada

Mahasanghika

Pataliputra (Patna)

Rajaghra

Bodh Gaya

VANGA

Sammatiya

AVANTI

Vidisha (Bhilsa)

Ujjain

Mahismati

Narmada R.

Tamralipti

Valabhi

APARANTA

Mahasasaka

MAHARASHTRA

Godavari R.

Mahamadi R.

KALINGA

ARABIAN SEA

BAY OF BENGAL

Krishna R.

Mahasanghika

VANAVASA

MAHISA MANDALA

SIMHALADVIPA/LANKA

Anuradhapura

SIMHALA (SRI LANKA)

Mahagama

INDIAN OCEAN

Miles
0   100   200

0 100 200 300
Kilometers

From the time of Ashoka, Buddhism began to travel further, according to tradition arriving in Sri Lanka. It later spread into South-East Asia, arriving in China via the Central Asian trade routes during the early centuries CE, spreading to Korea and other countries of East Asia, and reaching Japan in the 6th century CE. Buddhism came to Tibet by various routes, including India and China, probably from about the 7th century CE.

In India itself, for various reasons not yet fully understood – but possibly partly due to the rise of devotional theistic forms of Hinduism and the impact of Islam – Buddhism declined, almost ceasing to exist from about the 14th century CE.

It is common, but misleading, to speak of the Buddhism of China, Japan, and Tibet, as Mahayana, as opposed to the Theravada Buddhism of, for example, South-East Asia: but as stated earlier, they are not comparable phenomena. Nevertheless, many Mahayana scriptures were transmitted to, and usually given unquestioned authority in, China, Japan, and Tibet. Unlike in South-East Asia, Buddhists in these countries could be expected to express adherence to the Mahayana vision as embracing their highest aspirations.

Zen

Particularly characteristic of East Asian Buddhism is the tradition known in Japan as 'Zen'. Zen – the word is related to 'meditation' – stresses direct, non-verbal, intuitive insight, expressed through arts such as painting, but sometimes it also employs humour and shock to bring about awakening.

Also important in Japanese Buddhism is the 13th-century tradition of Shinran. For Shinran, the awakening of a Buddha is beyond the capability of the unenlightened; only by completely letting go of self-reliance and trusting in the Buddha's power to save can the already-enlightened nature of the Buddha (a Buddha known here as Amida) shine forth. Humans must let go of the egoism that encourages them to think they can achieve anything spiritually worthwhile – including enlightenment – through their own efforts. Being a monk or nun – or even meditating – is ultimately an irrelevant distraction and possible source of egoistic attachment.

Tantra and Vajrayana

From the beginning Buddhists accepted magic – bringing about desired results through the manipulation of hidden forces, usually by ritual means such as sacred circles (mandalas), utterances of power (mantras), and visualization. In addition to teaching, Buddhist monks and nuns might be asked by the lay communities that supported them to perform magic rituals for crops, health, and children. From early times, Buddhist ritual texts were produced, usually called tantras, and sometimes controversially attributed to the Buddha himself. Gradually the more disputed aspects of Tantric Buddhism were diluted and absorbed into the wider Mahayana context of compassion and wisdom. Such forms of tantra are found in Tibetan Buddhism.

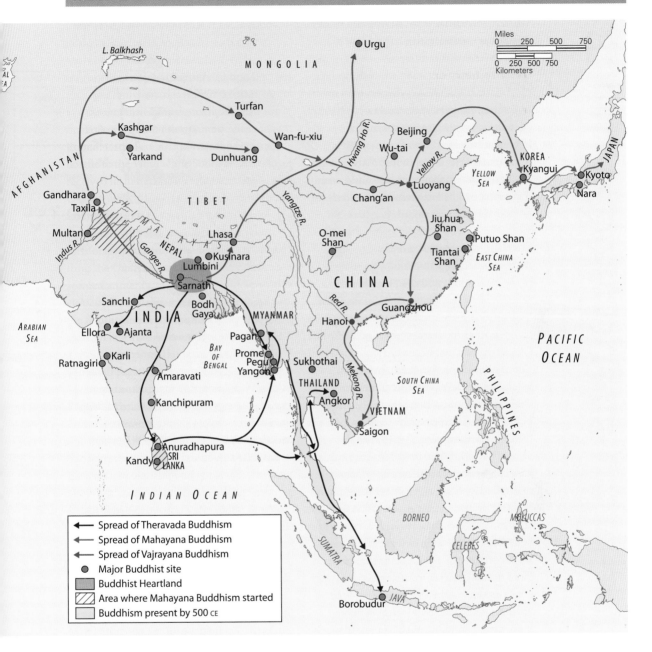

Miles
0 250 500 750

0 250 500 750
Kilometers

L. Balkhash

MONGOLIA

Urgu

Turfan

Kashgar

Wan-fu-xiu

Beijing

Wu-tai

Yarkand

Dunhuang

Yellow R.

KOREA

Kyangui

JAPAN

AFGHANISTAN

Hwang Ho R.

Luoyang

YELLOW
SEA

Kyoto

Gandhara

TIBET

Chang'an

Nara

Taxila

Jiu hua
Shan

Multan

Lhasa

O-mei
Shan

Putuo Shan

Indus R.

NEPAL

Ganges R.

Kusinara

Tiantai
Shan

EAST CHINA
SEA

Lumbini

CHINA

Sarnath

Sanchi

Bodh
Gaya

Red R.

INDIA

MYANMAR

Guangzhou

PACIFIC
OCEAN

ARABIAN
SEA

Ellora

Ajanta

Pagan

Hanoi

Karli

BAY
OF
BENGAL

Prome

Sukhothai

Ratnagiri

Pegu
Yangon

THAILAND

SOUTH CHINA
SEA

PHILIPPINES

Amaravati

Mekong R.

Kanchipuram

Angkor

VIETNAM

Saigon

Anuradhapura

Kandy

SRI
LANKA

INDIAN OCEAN

SUMATRA

BORNEO

MOLUCCAS

CELEBES

Borobudur

JAVA

← Spread of Theravada Buddhism
← Spread of Mahayana Buddhism
← Spread of Vajrayana Buddhism
● Major Buddhist site
▓ Buddhist Heartland
▨ Area where Mahayana Buddhism started
░ Buddhism present by 500 CE

During the European colonial period, Western visitors to South-East Asia started to study Buddhism, leading to a more text-based interpretation of the religion in the West. Meanwhile Asian Buddhism underwent a revival, as it strove to resist Christian missionary activity.

Sri Lanka, for instance, saw the development of 'Protestant Buddhism' – a form of Buddhism that protested against Christianity but also borrowed elements from it. Myanmar witnessed a similar revivalist development. At the beginning of the 20th century, Chinese Buddhism also underwent revival, though its impact was lessened by the growth of secular ideologies.

Secular ideologies and authoritarianism

In the mid-20th century, Buddhism in Cambodia, China, Korea, Laos, Tibet, and Vietnam was repressed by Communist regimes. After the establishment of the People's Republic of China in 1949, Chinese Communist leaders expected Buddhism would die away. When it did not, violent attacks on Buddhist leaders and religious buildings were instigated, particularly during the Cultural Revolution (1966–76).

British withdrawal from India in 1947 gave Communist China the opportunity to invade Tibet, in 1950. In 1959 the Buddhist leader, the Dalai Lama, fled the country and China imposed direct rule. Systematic suppression of Tibet's Buddhist heritage followed, including the looting of monasteries, destruction of libraries and religious images, and execution of monks. Thousands of Tibetans fled the country, mostly going to India, Nepal, and Bhutan, but some travelling as far as Europe and North America, spreading Tibetan forms of Buddhism.

Cambodia gained independence from France in 1953. In 1975, the capital, Phnom Penh, fell to the Khmer Rouge –

the Communist Party of Kampuchea – after which Buddhism was systematically dismantled. Buddhist temples were razed, monks killed, and libraries destroyed. After 1979, the people of Cambodia attempted to reconstruct its Buddhist heritage, donating money and rebuilding *wats* (temples). Buddhism was recognized as the state religion in 1989.

Today most schools of Buddhism are present in the West, and new Buddhist organizations have emerged to meet the needs of Westerners. In Britain, for example, Theravada Buddhism has a strong presence, with monasteries and educational centres catering both for Buddhists from Sri Lanka, Thailand, Myanmar, and for Western converts. Japanese Mahayana schools such as Zen, Pure Land, and Tendai are also represented – as are newer lay movements such as Soka Gakkai and Rissho Kosei-kai. Reacting to the suffering of the Vietnam War, the Zen Buddhist Thích Nhat Hanh (b. 1926) tried to apply Buddhist meditation practice and teaching to instances of political, economic, and environmental injustice and suffering in a movement known as 'Engaged Buddhism'. Engaged Buddhists believe meditation and social engagement should go hand in hand, and set up meditation centres for laypeople in Asia and the West. In traditional Asian Buddhism, meditation practices were linked with monastic life: today in Sri Lanka, Thailand, the USA, and Europe meditation has become an important part of life for laypeople too.

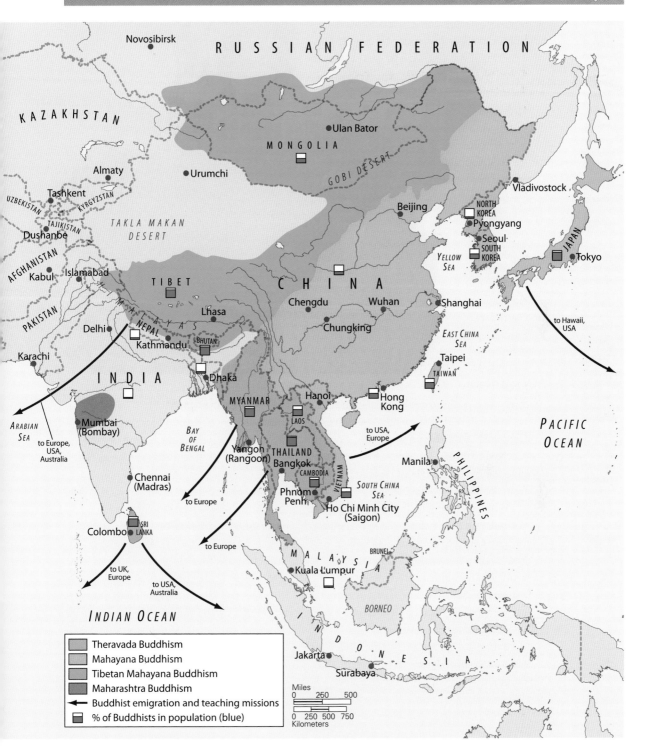

Novosibirsk

R U S S I A N   F E D E R A T I O N

K A Z A K H S T A N

•Ulan Bator

M O N G O L I A

Almaty

Urumchi

GOBI DESERT

Vladivostock

Tashkent

UZBEKISTAN

KYRGYZSTAN

TAKLA MAKAN
DESERT

Beijing

NORTH
KOREA
Pyongyang

TAJIKISTAN

Dushanbe

Seoul
SOUTH
KOREA

YELLOW
SEA

JAPAN

AFGHANISTAN

Kabul

Islamabad

T I B E T

C H I N A

Chengdu

Wuhan

Tokyo

Delhi

H I M A L A Y A S

NEPAL

Lhasa

Chungking

Shanghai

PAKISTAN

Kathmandu

BHUTAN

EAST CHINA
SEA

Karachi

Dhaka

Taipei

I N D I A

TAIWAN

ARABIAN
SEA

Mumbai
(Bombay)

to Europe,
USA,
Australia

BAY
OF
BENGAL

MYANMAR

Hanoi

Hong
Kong

LAOS

Chennai
(Madras)

to Europe

Yangon
(Rangoon)

THAILAND
Bangkok

to USA,
Europe

Manila

PACIFIC
OCEAN

PHILIPPINES

CAMBODIA

VIETNAM

SRI
LANKA

Colombo

to UK,
Europe

to Europe

Phnom
Penh

SOUTH CHINA
SEA

Ho Chi Minh City
(Saigon)

to USA,
Australia

INDIAN OCEAN

MALAYSIA

BRUNEI

Kuala Lumpur

BORNEO

I N D O N E S I A

to Hawaii,
USA

▨	Theravada Buddhism
▨	Mahayana Buddhism
▨	Tibetan Mahayana Buddhism
▨	Maharashtra Buddhism
←	Buddhist emigration and teaching missions
▥	% of Buddhists in population (blue)

Miles
0   250   500

0   250 500 750
Kilometers

Jakarta

Surabaya

Confucianism

Confucianism is best known for its moral philosophy, represented by the thinkers Confucius (551–479 BCE), Mencius (371– c. 289 BCE), and Hsün-tzu (fl. 298–238 BCE). Although grounded in religion – the ancient religion of the Lord-on-high, or Heaven – Confucianism gives primary emphasis to the ethical meaning of human relationships.

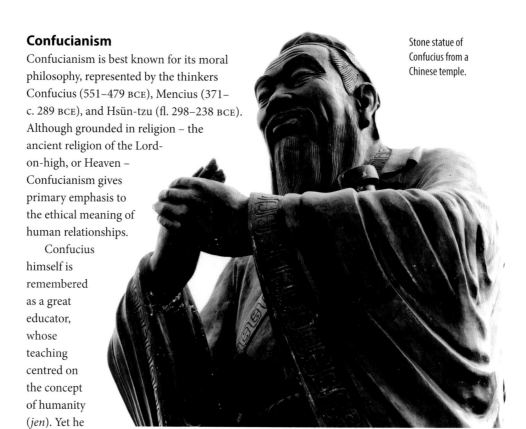

Stone statue of Confucius from a Chinese temple.

Confucius himself is remembered as a great educator, whose teaching centred on the concept of humanity (*jen*). Yet he made it clear that Heaven protected him and gave him his message. Within a few hundred years of Confucius' death, his principles had been accepted as the basis for social and political organization in China, and remained in place for more than two thousand years.

What was an implicitly religious message in Confucius becomes explicit in Mencius, who attempted to show how the Way of Heaven, the divine power of the cosmos, could become human nature. If human nature is correctly cultivated and nurtured, even the ordinary person can become a sage.

The third founding father of Confucianism, Hsün-tzu, is remembered for his doctrine of ritual action (*li*). He presents the practical side of Confucian religion, demonstrating the power of correct ritual action to transform the human heart – which is prone to err – into the mind of a sage.

Neo-Confucianism

Confucian mysticism, and particularly the later Neo-Confucianism, tend toward pantheism, as in the thought of Chang Tsai (1020–77), which is influenced by both Taoism and Buddhism. In his mystical vision, the entire world is related to him as his own family. Other Neo-Confucian thinkers include Chu Hsi (1130–1200) and Wang Yang-ming (1472–1529), whose schools were called respectively 'the teaching of principle' (*li-hsüeh*) and 'the teaching of mind' (*hsin-hsüeh*). Both were concerned with achieving sagehood: the debate between them concerned how to do this. Chu Hsi believed we have to go through an arduous process of self-cultivation and ethical activity to reach *jen*. But for Wang, only an 'enlightenment experience', uniting our minds with the mind of the Tao, can achieve sagehood.

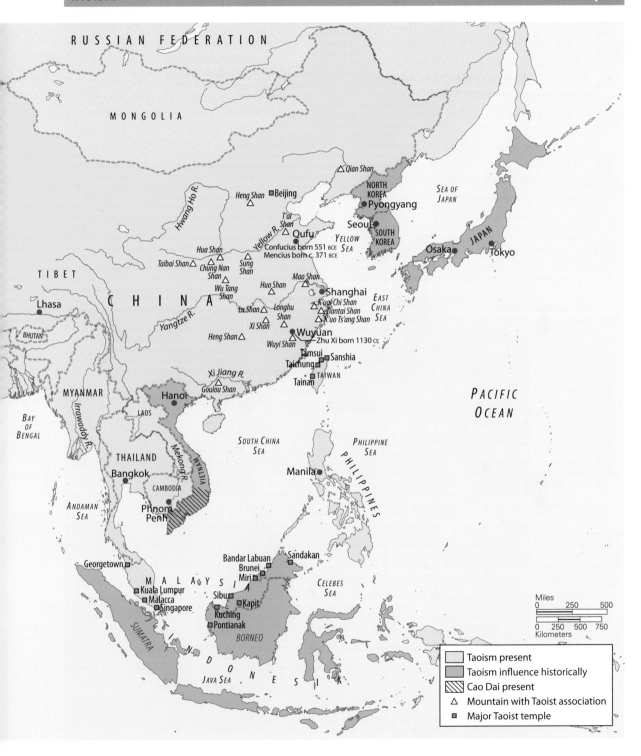

RUSSIAN FEDERATION

MONGOLIA

△ Qian Shan

Heng Shan ■ Beijing
△

NORTH
KOREA
● Pyongyang

SEA OF
JAPAN

*T'ai
Shan*
△ Qufu
Confucius born 551 BCE
Mencius born c. 371 BCE

● Seoul
SOUTH
KOREA

YELLOW
SEA

JAPAN

● Osaka
JAPAN
● Tokyo

Hua Shan △

Taibai Shan △ *Chung Nan
Shan* △ *Sung
Shan* △

Hwang Ho R.

Yellow R.

TIBET

C H I N A

*Wu Tang
Shan* △

Huo Shan △

Mao Shan △

● Shanghai

EAST
CHINA
SEA

● Lhasa

BHUTAN

Yangtze R.

Lu Shan △ *Longhu
Shan* △

Xi Shan △

K'uai Chi Shan △
Nantai Shan △
K'uo Ts'ang Shan △

Heng Shan △

△ Wuyuan
Zhu Xi born 1130 CE

Wuyi Shan △

Tamsui ■
Sanshia ■
Taichung ■

TAIWAN

Tainan ■

Xi Jiang R.

Goulou Shan △

PACIFIC
OCEAN

MYANMAR

Hanoi ●
LAOS

Irrawaddy R.

BAY
OF
BENGAL

THAILAND

Mekong R.

Bangkok ●

CAMBODIA

VIETNAM

SOUTH CHINA
SEA

PHILIPPINE
SEA

P H I L I P P I N E S

● Manila

ANDAMAN
SEA

Phnom
Penh ●

Bandar Labuan ■
Brunei ■
Miri ■

Sandakan ■

CELEBES
SEA

Georgetown ■

Kuala Lumpur ■
Malacca ■
Singapore ■

M A L A Y S I A

Sibu ■
Kapit ■

Kuching ■
Pontianak ■

BORNEO

SUMATRA

I
N
D
O
N
E
S
I
A

Java Sea

Miles
0   250   500

0   250   500   750
Kilometers

	Taoism present
	Taoism influence historically
	Cao Dai present
△	Mountain with Taoist association
■	Major Taoist temple

The Neo-Confucians gave Confucianism a fresh lease of life, offering a new explanation of the Confucian vision that could compete with Taoism and Buddhism. Both Hsi and Wang sought the moment when the human mind would be transformed into the Mind of Heaven, the state of perfected excellence.

Taoism

The Tao – a metaphysical absolute – seems to have been a philosophical transformation of an earlier personal God. The way it teaches leads to a union with itself – a way of passive acceptance and mystical contemplation. Such is the teaching of the great Taoist thinkers, Lao-tzu and Chuang-tzu, about whose lives little is known – if indeed they ever existed.

But Taoism is not mere passive contemplation. The texts of Lao-tzu and Chuang-tzu were utilized by a later generation of religious-minded thinkers, whose ambition was to 'steal the secret of Heaven and Earth', wrestle from it the mystery of life, and fulfil their desire for immortality. The goal of the Taoists was to become immortal (*hsien*). They revived belief in personal deities, practised a ritual of prayer, explored alchemy, and sought their goal through yoga and meditation.

This development in Taoism has been called 'Taoist religion', distinguishing it from the classical philosophy of Lao-tzu and Chuang-tzu. This Taoist religion developed its own mystical tradition, with stories of amazing drugs and miracle-working

The Hall of Prayer in the Taoist Temple of Heaven, Beijing, China.

immortals, levitations, and bodily ascents to heaven. Using early texts, the Taoist religionists created long-lasting institutions. Some of these groups still exist, tracing their roots back to Taoist movements of the late 2nd century CE. With their esoteric teachings, orthodox teachers, and social organizations, they resemble other great religious traditions, seeking unity with the Tao that cannot be named.

A major goal of all forms of Taoism was the quest for freedom: freedom from political and social constraints; a profound search for immortality; and a search for oneness with the Tao – the principle of the universe, and a pattern for human behaviour, but never a conscious god.

Throughout its history, the masters of Taoism have sought, in various ways, to become part of the 'self-so-ness' of reality. Taoist religion recognizes that life is a beautiful – and frightening – panorama of transformations. In their mountain retreats and lake pavilions, Taoists have been poets of nature.

Syncretism

The great Chinese religions have always influenced each other's development. Both Taoism and Confucianism borrowed a great deal from Buddhism, with the Taoists reforming their religious structures, founding monasteries, and writing a canon of sacred texts in imitation of Buddhist models.

The heyday of religious cross-fertilization in China came during the Ming dynasty (1369–1644), when many religious thinkers, such as Lin Chao-en (1517–98), sought to harmonize the three great religions, declaring that they are one. Lin sought to combine the best features of Taoist and Buddhist meditation with a Confucian sense of shared concern for fellow creatures, in a uniquely Chinese religious synthesis, still present in China today. Most religious Chinese are a mixture of all three great religions: Chinese syncretism has been so successful at blending traditions that few in China today would think it odd to be simultaneously Buddhist, Taoist, and Confucian.

Part 4

Judaism

According to the Old Testament account, Abraham's grandson Jacob (or 'Israel') had twelve sons – the original 'children of Israel'. These forefathers of Israel's twelve tribes spent their last years and died not in Canaan – the Promised Land – but in Egypt, driven there by famine.

Jacob's son Joseph became a senior administrator in Egypt and died there. 'A new king, who did not know about Joseph, came to power in Egypt' (Exodus 1:8) and the Egyptians now used Israelites as slave labour.

An Israelite named Moses – brought up in the Egyptian court – fled for his life to the Sinai Peninsula. Near Mount Sinai God spoke to him from a burning bush, telling him he must rescue the people of Israel and bring them to the promised land. Moses was to go to pharaoh and demand his people's release.

Pharaoh refused his demands; only after ten terrible plagues did he finally consent and let the Israelites go. The route taken is debated. The traditional route runs from Ra'amses to Succoth, then north across the Red Sea, or 'Sea of Reeds', before turning south-east to Mount Sinai. The location of some places visited by the Israelites are equally uncertain. The traditional site of Mount Sinai is Jebel Musa; however, some scholars place it at Jebel Helal, north Sinai. In this case, the Israelites would have taken the Way to Shur, via Beersheba.

It took the Hebrews about three months to reach Mount Sinai, where they stayed for almost a year. Here God gave Israel the moral law, the Ten Commandments. God also gave instructions for the construction of a 'tabernacle', a sacred tent situated in a large courtyard, first erected on the anniversary of the Israelites' escape from Egypt. Soon after, the tabernacle was dismantled and the Israelites left Sinai.

Forty years elapsed between the exodus from Egypt and the entry into Canaan, many spent at the oasis of Kadesh-Barnea in the Wilderness of Zin. But the children of Israel also wandered south to Sinai again, then north and east through the rugged Edomite territory south of the Dead Sea. From here they could have followed the King's Highway, but the Edomites would not allow them across their territory, so they had to travel around it. To the north the Amorites blocked the King's Highway but were defeated in battle. Attempts by the King of Moab to overthrow Israel were also thwarted.

Israel now camped on the plains of Moab, close to the River Jordan, and Moses addressed his people for the last time, before dying at Mount Nebo (or Pisgah).

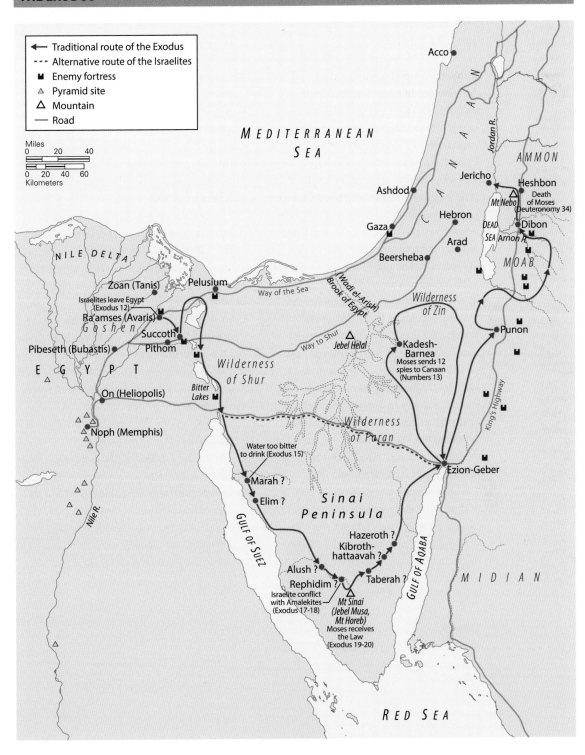

Legend:
- → Traditional route of the Exodus
- --- Alternative route of the Israelites
- ◪ Enemy fortress
- △ Pyramid site
- ▲ Mountain
- — Road

Miles
0   20   40

Kilometers
0   20   40   60

MEDITERRANEAN SEA

Acco

CANAAN

Jordan R.

AMMON

Ashdod

Jericho

Heshbon

Mt Nebo   Death of Moses (Deuteronomy 34)

Gaza

Hebron

DEAD SEA

Dibon

Arnon R.

NILE DELTA

Beersheba

Arad

MOAB

Way of the Sea

(Wadi el-Arish)
Brook of Egypt

Wilderness of Zin

Zoan (Tanis)

Pelusium

Israelites leave Egypt (Exodus 12)

Ra'amses (Avaris)

Goshen

Succoth

Pithom

Way to Shur

Jebel Helal

Kadesh-Barnea
Moses sends 12 spies to Canaan (Numbers 13)

Punon

Pibeseth (Bubastis)

EGYPT

King's Highway

On (Heliopolis)

Bitter Lakes

Wilderness of Shur

Wilderness of Paran

Noph (Memphis)

Water too bitter to drink (Exodus 15)

Marah ?

Elim ?

Sinai Peninsula

Ezion-Geber

Nile R.

GULF OF SUEZ

GULF OF AQABA

Hazeroth ?

Kibroth-hattaavah ?

Taberah ?

MIDIAN

Alush ?

Rephidim ?

Israelite conflict with Amalekites (Exodus 17-18)

Mt Sinai (Jebel Musa, Mt Horeb)
Moses receives the Law (Exodus 19-20)

RED SEA

For a period after the Israelites occupied Canaan, they were governed by a series of military leaders known in the Old Testament as 'judges'. The greatest of these was the prophet Samuel.

However Samuel displayed little military prowess, and during his rule the neighbouring Philistines captured the Israelites' holy Ark of the Covenant – the chest from the wilderness tabernacle that contained the sacred tablets of the Ten Commandments.

When Samuel grew old and appointed his sons judges, they took bribes and perverted justice. Neighbouring states were already kingdoms, and it was thought that Israel's military failures were due in part to her lack of leadership and unity. The elders of Israel demanded that Samuel appoint a king to govern them.

Saul

Israel's first king began his reign full of promise. Saul was rich, tall, young, and popular. He led Israel successfully against the Ammonites. In a series of assaults on Philistine garrisons, he achieved several victories over the old enemy. With the help of his son Jonathan, King Saul recorded a notable victory at Michmash.

Successful campaigns in the south prepared the way for Saul's successor, David, to enlarge his realm. However, Saul's jealousy of David – to the point of trying to kill him – marked a turn in his fortune. He and Jonathan died when Israel was defeated by the Philistines at the Battle of Gilboa.

David

David had been declared heir to the throne during Saul's lifetime, but spent the final years of Saul's reign in flight from him. He began his own reign in the city of Hebron, but later moved his capital to Jebus (captured from the Jebusites), changing its name to Jerusalem.

The Ark of the Covenant was now moved to this city.

David's capture of Jerusalem finally completed the Israelite conquest of Canaan. Having built a palace for himself in Jerusalem, David was anxious to build a house – or temple – for God. But a prophet forbade it, telling David that his son would be allowed to build this temple.

David now consolidated his kingdom: uniting his people, breaking the power of the Philistines, and expanding his frontiers with the Edomites, Ammonites, Moabites, and Arameans. He extended his kingdom to include lands from Dan in the north to the Brook of Egypt in the south, and his empire stretched much further, to the Euphrates river in the north and to Ezion-geber on the Gulf of Aqaba in the south. Edom, Moab, Ammon, and Aram all became his vassal states, forced to pay tribute.

Solomon

At his death, c. 970 BCE, David handed over to his son Solomon an empire that 50 years earlier would have been unimaginable, and whose size would not be seen again under Israelite rule. Solomon built a temple in his capital city, Jerusalem, where a complex system of animal sacrifices was carried out.

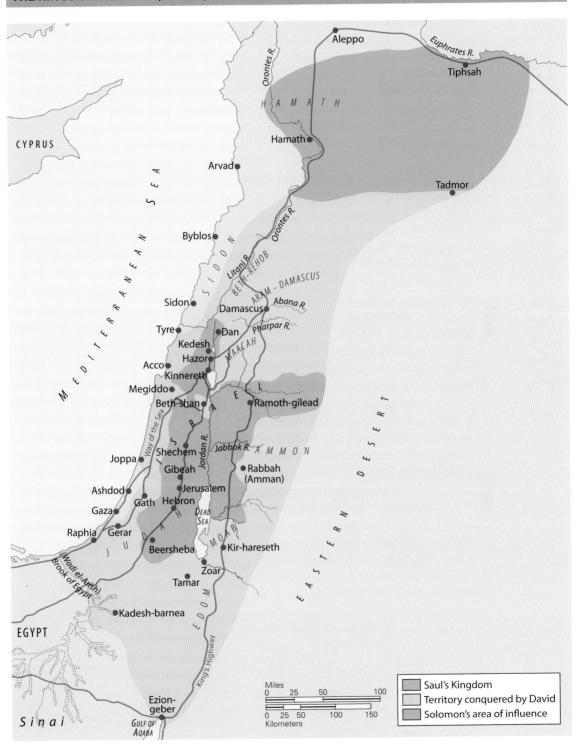

Miles
0   25   50   100

0 25 50   100   150
Kilometers

Saul's Kingdom
Territory conquered by David
Solomon's area of influence

Jewish Dispersions

The story of the early development of Judaism is much debated. The narrative based on the biblical books of Ezra and Nehemiah has been important for the development of Jewish self-understanding, but is not necessarily founded in historical reality.

In 586 BCE Nebuchadnezzar II, king of the neo-Babylonian Empire, destroyed Jerusalem and took many its people as captives to Babylon, along with much of the population of Judea.

In Babylon there was now a community of people who considered themselves Judeans, or Jews. They believed there should be a single temple in Jerusalem where religious sacrifice could be carried out. In an attempt to maintain continuity with the past, houses of assembly, 'synagogues' in Greek, were set up in Babylon. Here prayer, singing or chanting, teaching, and reading and discussion of the Torah took place. During this period, scribes also first appeared. Based in the synagogue, their role was to understand the Torah and interpret its rules for the contemporary situation. This 'guild of scholars' seems to have evolved into the rabbis of later rabbinic Judaism.

In 539 the army of Cyrus II 'the Great' of Persia captured Babylon. According to the book of Ezra, he permitted the Jews to return from exile and rebuild their temple in Jerusalem. When Jewish religious leaders returned to Jerusalem and rebuilt the Temple, the city was apparently established as a temple community led by the priests.

THE JEWISH EXILES

Aspendos

CYPR

CYPR

MEDITERRANEAN SEA

Alexandria

Daphn

EGYPT

Elephantine

Nile R.

Syene

Miles
0   50   100   150

0   50   100   200
Kilometers

map 20

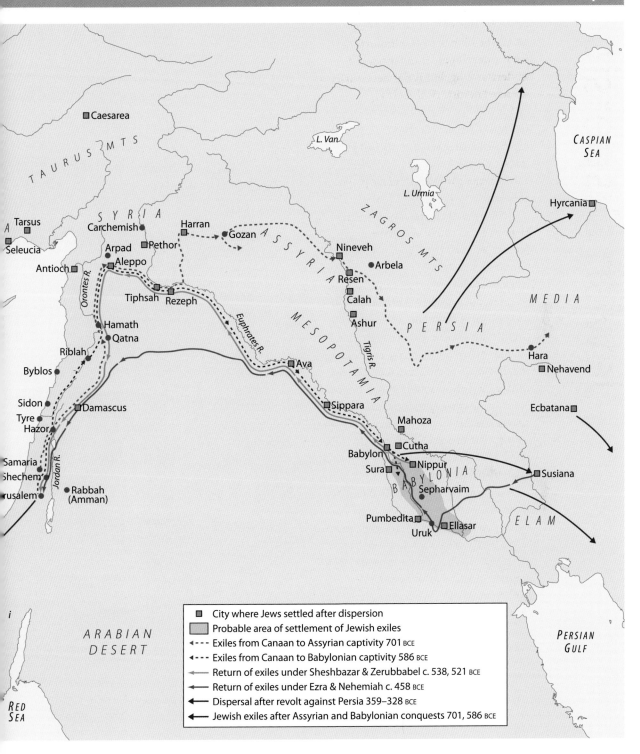

Caesarea

L. Van

CASPIAN
SEA

L. Urmia

ZAGROS MTS

Hyrcania

TAURUS MTS

SYRIA

Tarsus

Carchemish

Harran

Gozan

ASSYRIA

Nineveh

Arbela

MEDIA

Seleucia

Arpad

Pethor

Aleppo

Resen

Antioch

Orontes R.

Tiphsah

Rezeph

Euphrates R.

MESOPOTAMIA

Calah

Ashur

PERSIA

Hara

Nehavend

Hamath

Qatna

Tigris R.

Riblah

Byblos

Ava

Ecbatana

Sidon

Sippara

Tyre

Hazor

Damascus

Mahoza

Jordan R.

Samaria

Shechem

rusalem

Rabbah
(Amman)

Babylon

Cutha

Nippur

Sura

BABYLONIA

Sepharvaim

Susiana

Pumbedita

Uruk

Ellasar

ELAM

ARABIAN
DESERT

PERSIAN
GULF

RED
SEA

	City where Jews settled after dispersion
	Probable area of settlement of Jewish exiles
◄----	Exiles from Canaan to Assyrian captivity 701 BCE
◄----	Exiles from Canaan to Babylonian captivity 586 BCE
◄——	Return of exiles under Sheshbazar & Zerubbabel c. 538, 521 BCE
◄——	Return of exiles under Ezra & Nehemiah c. 458 BCE
◄——	Dispersal after revolt against Persia 359–328 BCE
◄——	Jewish exiles after Assyrian and Babylonian conquests 701, 586 BCE

NORTH
SEA

BRITANNIA

ATLANTIC
OCEAN

Noviomagus
Colonia Agrippina (Cologne)
Bonna (Bonn)
Augusta Treverorum (Trier)
Durocortorum
GERMANIA
Castra Regina
Lutetia
Cenabum Aureliani
Vesontio
GALLIA
NORICUM
Danube R.
Rhine R.
RAETIA
PANNONIA
SARMATIA
DACIA
Olbi

Mediolanum
(Milan)
Ravenna
Aquileia
Lugdunum (Lyons)
Rhône R.
Genoa
AQUITANIA
Tolosa (Toulouse)
Elimberris
Massilia
(Marseilles)
Arelate
Roma
(Rome)
ITALIA
Salonae
DALMATIA
Serdica
MOESIA
Oescus
MACEDONIA
THRACIA
Byzantium
Thessalonica
Nicomedia
Anc
Barium
Larisa
Pergamum
ASIA
Tarraco
(Tarragona)
HISPANIA
Neapolis (Naples)
Salernum
Tarentum
Thebae
Patrae
Corinth
Ephesus
Sparta
ACHA
Athens
Miletus
Emerita Augusta
Corduba
BAETICA
Carthago
Nova
Panormus
SICILIA
Carthago
Syracusae
CRETA
Gades
(Cadiz)
Caesarea
Cirta
NUMIDIA
Hadrumetum
MEDITERRANEAN SEA
Volubilis
MAURETANIA

AFRICA

Cyrene
Oea
Berenice
Alexandria
Pelus
LIBYA
Memphis

AEGYPTU

Nile

Dnieper R.

Legend

- ○ City with Jewish community by 300 CE
- ● City with large Jewish community by 300 CE
- ○ City with Jewish community by 400 CE
- Area of Jewish settlement by 300 CE
- Area of Jewish settlement by 400 CE
- — Roman Empire by c. 300 CE
- ← Jewish dispersion routes

Miles
0   100   200   300

0   200   400
Kilometers

map 21

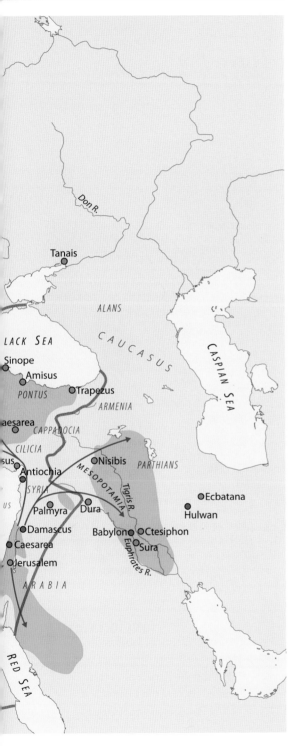

The Jewish Diaspora

Jewish dispersion (the 'Diaspora') started in the 6th century BCE, when many Jews opted to remain in Babylon, where they had been taken as exiles. From this time on, Jewish communities 'of the Diaspora' grew all around the Mediterranean Sea, focussing their religious observance around the local synagogue.

During the Roman period, Jewish hopes rose for a messiah who would rescue his people from the Roman occupiers and restore the Judean state. In 66 CE the Jews rose in revolt against Rome. Rome retook Jerusalem and destroyed its temple in 70 CE in a crushing defeat. No longer would Jerusalem be the destination of Jewish pilgrims or the centre of Jewish cultural life.

Galilee now became a centre of Jewish life. Johanan ben Zakai (30–90 CE) founded a school at Jamnia, or Yavneh, Galilee, where 'rabbi' (master) became the formal title for teachers. The school at Jamnia began to function as a Jewish council, discussing the meaning of the Jewish law. It is also held to have founded Rabbinic Judaism: the belief that, on Mount Sinai, Moses – the first rabbi – received from God the written law (the 'Torah', or Pentateuch) and an oral explanation (the 'oral Torah').

The Jewish community in Egypt remained quite strong, but Greek culture – and Hellenistic Judaism – was on the wane. In Babylon, the ruler of the Jews of the Diaspora was known as the 'exilarch', or head of the exiles, a hereditary position recognized by the state.

The conversion of the Roman Emperor Constantine to Christianity in 313 CE was inauspicious for Jews. Although Judaism was never actually proscribed, life for Jews became increasingly difficult.

Judaism and the Rise of Islam

In the 7th and 8th centuries CE Islam arose and spread with extraordinary rapidity. Muslim Arabs conquered Syria and Palestine in 634, defeated Persia in 637, and took Egypt soon after. In 711 they invaded Spain and set up a Muslim state. Within a single century, many Jews had come under Muslim rule.

For most Jews, living conditions improved. They also shared in the intellectual ferment of the Arab world. Arabs translated and studied the learning of Greece, Persia, China, and India. Drawing on these resources, Muslim and Jewish scholars made great advances in mathematics, astronomy, philosophy, chemistry, medicine, and philology. One of the greatest Jewish philosophers, Sa'adiah ben Yosef Gaon (882–942), grappled with the problem of faith and knowledge, discussing proofs of God's existence.

Babylon

In Babylon the authority and importance of the Gaons – heads of the Babylonian Jewish academies – grew immensely after 600 CE. The Gaons ensured that the Babylonian Talmud – religious documents compiled in the Babylonian academies between the 3rd and 5th centuries CE – became more widely accepted.

In the 9th century a gaonate was established in Palestine, and was recognized as authoritative by Jews in Spain, Egypt, and Italy. Under the Gaons collections of Talmudic laws were made, synagogue poetry written, prayer books drawn up, and the text of the Bible fixed and annotated. Most influential were the *Responsa* (Hebrew, *She'elot ve-Teshuvot* – questions and answers), questions on matters of religious practice sent to the Gaons, debated in the academies, and answered in their name.

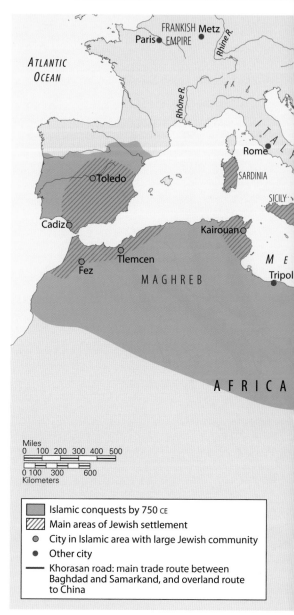

THE JEWS AND ISLAM c. 750 CE

Miles
0 100 200 300 400 500
0 100 300 600
Kilometers

- Islamic conquests by 750 CE
- Main areas of Jewish settlement
- City in Islamic area with large Jewish community
- Other city
- Khorasan road: main trade route between Baghdad and Samarkand, and overland route to China

Variants from rabbinic Judaism arose. In 8th century CE Babylon, Anan ben David (c. 715–c. 795) and the Karaite movement he possibly founded rejected the Talmud and all forms of oral law, such as the Mishnah, taking a stand on the Bible only. It seemed the

map 22

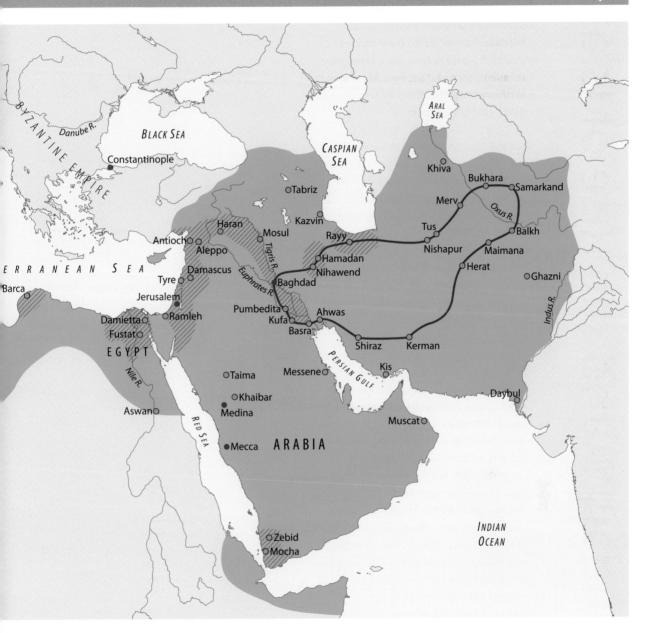

Karaites might divide the Jewish world, but
the movement rapidly dwindled into a sect,
which survives today in small numbers.

Anti-Semitism and Messianism

From the 10th century onwards, anti-Jewish sentiment and violence became increasingly frequent and bitter in Christian Europe. Lies about the Jews circulated, and the Jews were expelled from England in 1290, from France in 1306, and from Spain in 1492.

During the 16th and 17th centuries, the Muslim Ottoman Empire was in the ascendant, expanding into Europe until halted at Vienna in 1683. Most Jews now lived either in Christian Poland–Lithuania or under the Ottoman Empire, where conditions were generally less difficult, but where they were still subject to arbitrary acts by rulers. In Christian Italy, severe penalties were imposed on the Jews in this period.

From the early 17th century, Jews began to move from Poland and the Ottoman Empire into the cities of the West, where there was growing recognition of the value of Jewish commercial activity.

The Protestant Reformers on the whole favoured Jews, but Martin Luther moved from tolerance to anti-Jewish abuse. The rite of non-Sephardic Jews in Europe, especially Germany – known as 'Ashkenazi' – dates to the 16th century, and has its own German-Jewish dialect, Yiddish.

Anti-Jewish riots continued, but the authorities now more often protected the Jews, regarded as useful for their money-lending and trading. In Ukraine and Poland many Jews were killed in massacres in 1648 and 1649.

In the late 17th century a number of Jewish messianic movements arose. The most important centred on Shabbetai Zevi (1628–1716). The Jewish community regarded his followers with suspicion and the episode resulted in disillusion with messianism.

Jews had been expelled from England in 1290, but began to return in 1656 during Cromwell's protectorate.

Western Ashenazi Jews
Eastern Ashkenazi Jews
Sephardic Jews
Italian Jews (=Roman)
← Major Jewish migration
◇ Yeshivah (Rabbinic school)
▲ Karaite centre
■ Kabbalist or Sabbataean centre

BALTIC
SEA

Birzai

Vilna

Königsberg

PRUSSIA

Grodno   Trakal   Minsk

POLAND   Sluck

Hamburg

Poznan

Berlin

Warsaw   Brest-Litovsk

Amsterdam   Pinsk

NETHERLANDS

Dresden   Lublin

Cologne

Breslau   Ludmir   Kiev

Frankfurt   Lvov

Prague   Luck   Ostrog

Rhine R.   Krakov

Nickelsburg   Halicz   Derazne

Strasburg   Augsburg   Dnieper R.   Don R.

Danube R.   Vienna

Munich

AUSTRIA   Budapest

HUNGARY

Padua

Pavia   Venice

Rhône R.   Cremona   Mantua

Bucharest

Belgrade

Livorno   BLACK SEA

ITALY   Ulcini   Sofia

Rome   Edirne

Naples   Salonica   Constantinople

O T T O M A N   E M P I R E

M E D I T E R R A N E A N

Smyrna (Izmir)

S E A

Euphrates R.

Safed

Jerusalem

A F R I C A   Cairo

E G Y P T

Nile R.   RED
SEA

Miles
0   100   200   300   400   500

0   100   300   500   700
Kilometers

RUSSIA

ANTI-SEMITISM AND MESSIANISM   71

The writings of Moses Mendelssohn (1729–86), a German Jewish philosopher, led to the development of a Jewish Enlightenment, the *Haskalah*, that attempted to introduce the Jewish community to contemporary European thought and culture.

In 1781 the Holy Roman Emperor, Joseph II, issued an Edict of Toleration. In 1789 the revolutionary National Assembly of France declared that no religious opinion should be persecuted. In 1806 the Emperor Napoleon even summoned an Assembly of Jewish Notables.

These progressive tendencies were largely suppressed after the Napoleonic wars, but the rights of Jews continued to be asserted. By 1871 all restrictions had been removed in Germany, and Jews were declared full citizens of the newly unified Reich. The Scandinavian countries had only small Jewish populations, but full emancipation was accomplished in 1848 in Denmark, 1851 in Norway, and 1865 in Sweden.

The Netherlands was traditionally tolerant and Jewish rights had been established there early. Great Britain also had a longer history of tolerance; throughout the 19th century the Jewish community enjoyed commercial prosperity and civil respect. Yet full equal rights were not granted until 1890. Emancipation was achieved in the Austro-Hungarian Empire in 1867. But in Eastern Europe Jewish life continued much as it had during previous centuries. In Russia it took the 1917 Revolution and World War I for the Jews to attain full citizenship.

Emancipation also aided the assimilation of Jews – and sometimes their cultural disappearance, when they merged through marriage into the surrounding society.

Counter-intuitively, with increased tolerance came anti-Semitism, based on pseudo-scientific ideas of racial stereotypes. From the 1880s, anti-Semitic movements were promoted in Germany and France by such as Wilhelm Marr (1819–1904), who insisted on the racial distinction of Germans and Jews, and invented the term 'anti-Semitism'.

Interior of the Old Portuguese Synagogue, Amsterdam, known as the Esnoga or Snoge, opened in 1675.

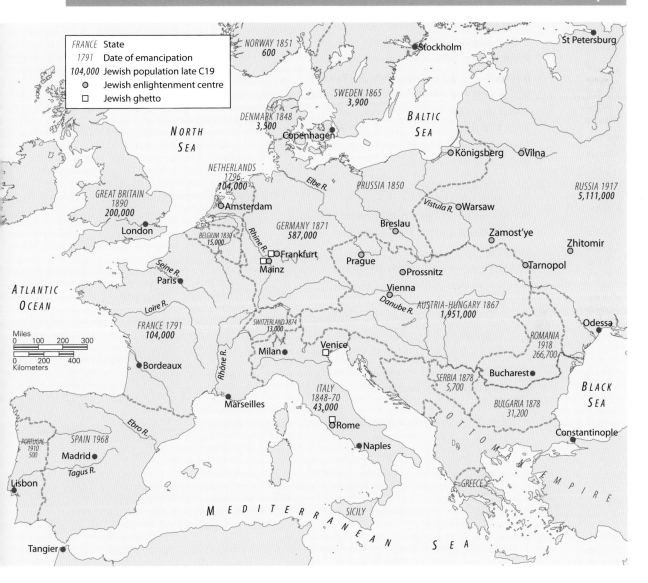

FRANCE   State
1791   Date of emancipation
104,000   Jewish population late C19
◉   Jewish enlightenment centre
▢   Jewish ghetto

NORWAY 1851
600

SWEDEN 1865
3,900

DENMARK 1848
3,500

NORTH
SEA

BALTIC
SEA

St Petersburg

Stockholm

Copenhagen

Königsberg   Vilna

NETHERLANDS
1796
104,000

GREAT BRITAIN
1890
200,000

Amsterdam

Elbe R.

PRUSSIA 1850

Vistula R.   Warsaw

RUSSIA 1917
5,111,000

London

BELGIUM 1830
15,000

GERMANY 1871
587,000

Breslau

Zamost'ye

Zhitomir

Rhine R.

Frankfurt

Prague

Tarnopol

Seine R.

Mainz

Prossnitz

ATLANTIC
OCEAN

Paris

Loire R.

Vienna

AUSTRIA-HUNGARY 1867
1,951,000

Odessa

FRANCE 1791
104,000

SWITZERLAND 1874
13,000

Danube R.

Miles
0   100   200   300

0   200   400
Kilometers

Rhône R.

Milan

Venice

ROMANIA
1918
266,700

Bordeaux

ITALY
1848-70
43,000

SERBIA 1878
5,700

Bucharest

BLACK
SEA

Marseilles

BULGARIA 1878
31,200

Rome

Ebro R.

PORTUGAL
1910
500

SPAIN 1968

Madrid

Naples

Constantinople

Lisbon

Tagus R.

GREECE

MEDITERRANEAN   SEA

SICILY

Tangier

Judaism in the USA

At the start of the 19th century many East European Jews in rural areas lived in a close-knit community known as a *shtetl*, a stockaded, traditional culture shut off from the secular world. However, as large numbers began to emigrate to the United States, initially attracted by business and social opportunities, Orthodox leaders such as Rabbi Samson Hirsch (1808–88) encouraged them to involve themselves in the culture of the Western world.

Reform Judaism originated in Germany, where the 18th century Enlightenment stressed reason and progress. Abraham Geiger (1810–74) and others declared that modern Jews could no longer accept the Torah as revealed truth, and encouraged changes in ritual law and worship. Dietary laws were abandoned, prayers were translated from Hebrew into the vernacular, and synagogue worship was changed. Some Jews even began to worship on Sunday rather than *Shabbat* (Saturday, the traditional Jewish Sabbath).

In the USA, the Reform movement was led by Isaac Wise (1819–1900), who in 1875 set up the Hebrew Union College in Cincinnati, Ohio, the main seminary for training Reform rabbis.

THE ORIGINS OF JUDAISM IN THE USA

map 25

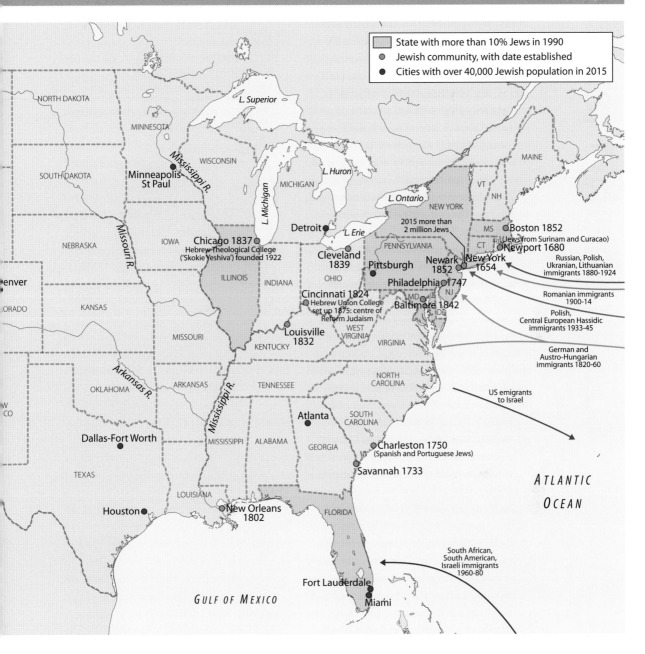

State with more than 10% Jews in 1990
Jewish community, with date established
Cities with over 40,000 Jewish population in 2015

NORTH DAKOTA

MINNESOTA

L. Superior

WISCONSIN

SOUTH DAKOTA

Minneapolis-St Paul

Mississippi R.

L. Michigan

MICHIGAN

L. Huron

MAINE

VT

NH

NEBRASKA

Missouri R.

IOWA

Chicago 1837
Hebrew Theological College
('Skokie Yeshiva') founded 1922

Detroit

L. Erie

Cleveland
1839

NEW YORK

L. Ontario

2015 more than
2 million Jews

MS

CT

RI

Boston 1852
Newport 1680
(Jews from Surinam and Curacao)

Russian, Polish,
Ukranian, Lithuanian
immigrants 1880-1924

enver

COLORADO

KANSAS

ILLINOIS

INDIANA

OHIO

PENNSYLVANIA

Pittsburgh

Newark
1852

New York
1654

Philadelphia 1747

NJ

Romanian immigrants
1900-14

Cincinnati 1824
Hebrew Union College
set up 1875: centre of
Reform Judaism

MD

Baltimore 1842

DE

Polish,
Central European Hassidic
immigrants 1933-45

W
CO

MISSOURI

Louisville
1832

WEST
VIRGINIA

KENTUCKY

VIRGINIA

German and
Austro-Hungarian
immigrants 1820-60

Arkansas R.

OKLAHOMA

ARKANSAS

TENNESSEE

NORTH
CAROLINA

US emigrants
to Israel

NW
CO

Mississippi R.

MISSISSIPPI

ALABAMA

Atlanta

SOUTH
CAROLINA

GEORGIA

Charleston 1750
(Spanish and Portuguese Jews)

TEXAS

Dallas-Fort Worth

Savannah 1733

ATLANTIC
OCEAN

LOUISIANA

Houston

New Orleans
1802

FLORIDA

South African,
South American,
Israeli immigrants
1960-80

Fort Lauderdale

GULF OF MEXICO

Miami

The Holocaust

In 1933, Adolf Hitler (1889–1945), leader of the NSDAP – *Nationalsozialistische Deutsche Arbeiterpartei*, the Nazi Party – was appointed German Chancellor amid the economic disaster of the Great Depression. Once in power, the Nazi Party suspended the constitution, eliminated other political parties, outlawed strikes, and staged book-burnings. In 1934 the role of Hitler's elite security force, the SS, was expanded under Heinrich Himmler (1900–45), taking over many police functions as well as running the concentration camps.

Jewish academics and professionals lost their jobs, Jewish shops were boycotted, and Jews were prevented from participating in civic life. In 1935, the Nuremberg Laws deprived Jews of their citizenship and criminalized sexual relationships between Jews and non-Jews. In 1938 Jewish communal bodies were put under the control of the Gestapo secret police. On 9 November 1938, '*Kristallnacht*', the Nazis organized an onslaught against the Jewish population, killing, looting, and setting fire to homes, schools, shops, and 250 synagogues.

When the Nazis invaded Poland in 1939, at the start of World War II, Germans forced Jews to hand over jewellery, clear rubble, carry heavy loads, and scrub floors and lavatories with their prayer shawls. After the German invasion of Russia in 1941, the Nazis began carrying out what they euphemistically termed 'the final solution to the Jewish problem': the extermination of European Jews. Following Hitler's orders, mobile task forces called *Einsatzgruppen* – killing squads under the command of Reinhard Heydrich (1904–42) – began systematically to murder the Jews of Russia and Eastern Europe. Of 4,500,000 Jews who lived in Soviet territory, more than half fled before the invasion;

Germany in 1937
'Greater Germany' in 1942
Territory occupied by Germany
Axis power or occupied by Axis power
Jewish Ghetto
Concentration camp or slave-labour camp
Extermination camp
Site of mass murder
European borders in 1937

NORTH SEA

IRELAND
5,000
4,500

UNITED KINGDOM
340,000
350,000

London

BELGIU
44,00
24,00
30,00

Alderney

Dran
Seine R.
Paris

ATLANTIC OCEAN

FRANCE
270,000
83,000
180,000

Gurs   Noë

Ebro R.

PORTUGAL
3,000
4,000

Madrid

SPAIN
5,000
3,500

Miles
0   100   200   300

0   100 200   400
Kilometers

map 26

FINLAND
2,000
1,800

NORWAY
2,000
870
1,000

SWEDEN
10,000
22,000

Klooga

ESTONIA
5,000
1,000
500

Vaivara

LATVIA
94,000
80,000
12,000

Riga
Kaiserwald

RUSSIA

LITHUANIA
160,000
135,000
20,000

Kaunas

Moscow

DENMARK
7,000
120
5,500

BALTIC
SEA

Vilna

HERLANDS
115,000
06,000
30,000

Neuengamme

Stutthof

POLAND
3,275,000
4,565,000
(with Lithuania)
120,000

Ponary

Minsk
Trostenets

Ravensbrück
Sachsenhausen

Bialystok

Treblinka

Bergen-Belsen

Berlin

Warsaw

Westerbork
sterdam

Niederhagen

Chelm

Lodz

Sobibor

zogenbusch
chelen
Dora
Mittelbau

Bernburg

Gross Rosen

Lublin

Majdanek

Buchenwald

Rhine R.

GERMANY
365,000
125,000
85,000

Theresienstadt

Czestochawa
Sosnoviec

Krakow-
Plaszow

Belzek

Brody

Kiev

LUX.
3,000
700
500

Prague

Auschwitz

Strysnow

Lvov

Babi-Yar

Flossenberg

Brno

Natzweiler-
Struthof

Mauthausen

Nitra

CZECHOSLOVAKIA
360,000 – **277,000**
55,000

Bar

Balanowka

Dachau

Danube R.

Bogdanovka

AUSTRIA
180,000 – **70,000**
16,000

Budapest

Edineti

Odessa

SWITZERLAND
20,000
35,000

HUNGARY
440,000 – **300,000**
200,000

ROMANIA
800,000
264,000
300,000

Jasenovac

Gospic

Zemun

Sajmiste

YUGOSLAVIA
75,000
60,000
10,500

ITALY
50,000
7,500
52,000

Les Milles

ADRIATIC SEA

Sofia

BULGARIA
50,000
46,500

BLACK SEA

Rome

MEDITERRANEAN

GREECE
75,000
65,000
10,500

TURKEY
75,000
80,000

SEA

GERMANY — Country
365,000 — Jews pre-war
125,000 — Approx number of Jews killed
85,000 — Numbers of Jews post war

THE HOLOCAUST   77

those who remained were concentrated in restricted areas of large cities ('ghetttos'). *Einsatzgruppen* rounded them up, took them to the woods, and machine-gunned them to death. In early 1942, senior Nazis met at Wannsee, on the outskirts of Berlin, to coordinate plans for the murder of up to 11 million Jews. Central to their strategy was the network of death camps at Chelmno, Auschwitz-Birkenau, Treblinka, Sobibor, Majdanek, and Belzec. At Auschwitz, the largest of these camps, the first gassing had taken place in September 1941.

By September 1942, Germany had conquered most of Europe. But as the murder of Jews continued, resistance grew. In the Warsaw ghetto, the Jewish Fighting Organization retaliated. However 7,000 Jews lost their lives in the fighting, and 30,000 more were deported to Treblinka. The murders continued across Europe. In the summer of 1944 the last deportations took place, when more than 67,000 were sent from the Lodz ghetto to Birkenau. Most victims were sent to the gas chamber, but some were chosen for inhuman medical experiments. By the end of the war, more than 6 million Jews had lost their lives in the most terrible circumstances imaginable.

In the years since, the Jewish community has struggled with the religious perplexity of the Holocaust: where was God at Jewry's time of dire need? These terrible events are commemorated today on Holocaust Memorial Days and in Holocaust memorials and museums throughout the world, such as *Yad va-Shem* in Israel.

Zionism

Theodore Herzl (1860–1904), an Austro-Hungarian Jewish journalist, came to believe the Jews needed a homeland of their own as a refuge from the growing anti-Semitism in 19th century Europe, and began to campaign to bring such a Jewish state into existence.

Earlier in the 19th century, Jewish pioneers had already started to return to Palestine, living mostly in four holy cities: Hebron, Jerusalem, Safed, and Tiberias. Some such 'Zionists' ignored the problem that there was already an indigenous Palestinian Arab population; others believed Jews and Arabs could co-exist and develop the land together.

The need for a state where Jews could escape persecution was drastically demonstrated by the Holocaust. As the enormity of Nazi crimes was revealed, the Zionist cause gained new momentum. Since 1920, Palestine had been governed by the British, under a League of Nations mandate.

In May 1947, the United Nations decided that Palestine should now be partitioned into a Jewish state and an Arab state. On 14 May 1948, the independence of the Jewish State of Israel was declared by the United Nations. Palestinian refugees fled their homes in Israeli-held territory, many sheltering in refugee camps. The Israeli War of Independence continued throughout 1948, and conflict re-occurred in 1954, in 1967, and 1973.

Following the Six Day War (1967), between neighbouring Arab states and Israel, Israel took possession of territories previously allotted to Arab countries by the United Nations. Since that time, these 'occupied territories' have roused Jewish-Arab tensions, with Israel seeing them as vital to their national security, and the Arabs striving to regain political dominance.

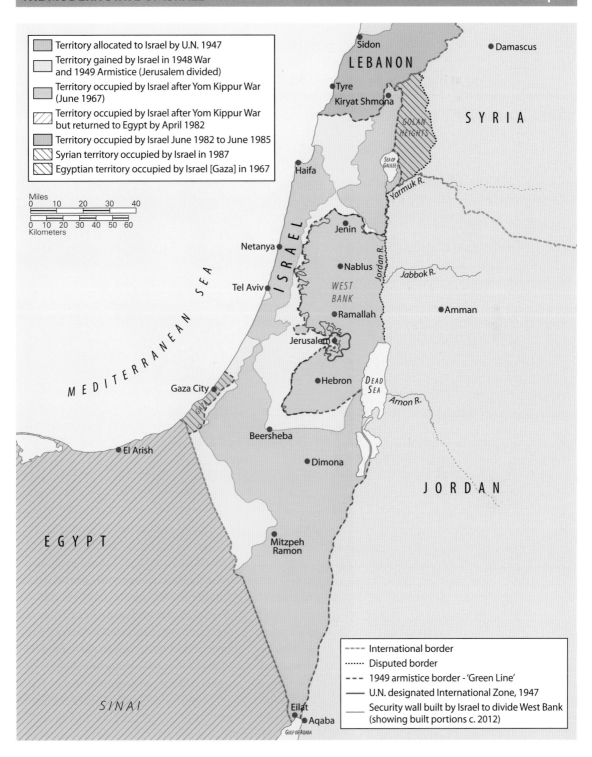

Legend:

- Territory allocated to Israel by U.N. 1947
- Territory gained by Israel in 1948 War and 1949 Armistice (Jerusalem divided)
- Territory occupied by Israel after Yom Kippur War (June 1967)
- Territory occupied by Israel after Yom Kippur War but returned to Egypt by April 1982
- Territory occupied by Israel June 1982 to June 1985
- Syrian territory occupied by Israel in 1987
- Egyptian territory occupied by Israel [Gaza] in 1967

Miles
0 10 20 30 40

0 10 20 30 40 50 60
Kilometers

---- International border

..... Disputed border

- - - 1949 armistice border - 'Green Line'

—— U.N. designated International Zone, 1947

—— Security wall built by Israel to divide West Bank (showing built portions c. 2012)

Map labels: Sidon, Damascus, LEBANON, Tyre, Kiryat Shmona, SYRIA, GOLAN HEIGHTS, SEA OF GALILEE, Haifa, Yarmuk R., Jenin, Netanya, ISRAEL, Nablus, Jordan R., Jabbok R., Tel Aviv, WEST BANK, Ramallah, Amman, Jerusalem, MEDITERRANEAN SEA, Hebron, DEAD SEA, Arnon R., Gaza City, GAZA, Beersheba, Dimona, JORDAN, El Arish, EGYPT, Mitzpeh Ramon, SINAI, Eilat, Aqaba, GULF OF AQABA

Part 5

Christianity

In 40 BCE Herod the Great, who had been military prefect of Galilee and joint tetrarch of Judea, was made 'king of the Jews' by the Roman senate. Soon after, the Parthians invaded Syria and Palestine and installed their own king. However, Herod gradually reconquered his kingdom, and in 37 BCE captured Jerusalem, executing Antigonus, the last of the Maccabean priest-rulers. Thereby he secured the throne for himself until his death in 4 BCE, when the kingdom was divided among his three sons.

Although a Jew by religion, Herod was very unpopular. He strongly supported Roman policy, even erecting shrines to pagan gods. As well as building several cities and fortresses outside Jerusalem, Herod made major additions to the city, such as the Temple Mount, the Antonia Fortress, and the Upper Palace. In 19 BCE reconstruction of the temple commenced, work that continued almost until 70 CE, when the temple was again and finally destroyed, this time by the Romans.

Upon the death of Herod, Palestine became a province ruled by his sons as 'tetrarchs', provincial rulers subject to Rome. Archelaus, 'Herod the Ethnarch', ruled Judea from 4 BCE to 6 CE, when he was exiled by the Romans for misgovernment. A Roman governor or 'procurator' then ruled Judea until 41 CE. Herod Antipas ruled Galilee and part of Transjordan from 4 BCE to 39 CE, while Herod Philip ruled the northern regions until 34 CE.

The Decapolis was a confederation of ten cities formed after the Roman general Pompey's campaign (65–62 BCE). It gave protection to its Gentile citizens, who were mainly Greek-speaking Roman soldiers, against both militant Jews and Arabian tribes.

Remains of the aqueduct built under Herod the Great at Caesarea Maritima.

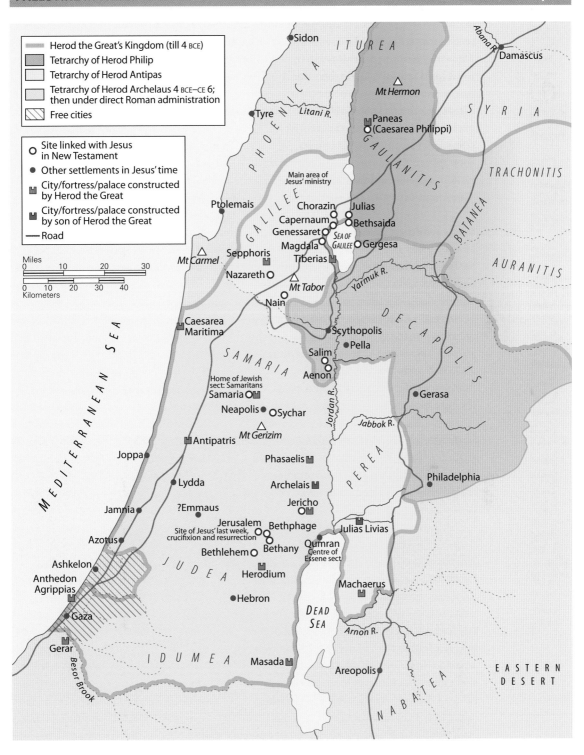

Legend:

- Herod the Great's Kingdom (till 4 BCE)
- Tetrarchy of Herod Philip
- Tetrarchy of Herod Antipas
- Tetrarchy of Herod Archelaus 4 BCE–CE 6; then under direct Roman administration
- Free cities

- ○ Site linked with Jesus in New Testament
- ● Other settlements in Jesus' time
- City/fortress/palace constructed by Herod the Great
- City/fortress/palace constructed by son of Herod the Great
- — Road

Miles
0   10   20   30

0   10   20   30   40
Kilometers

Map labels:

Sidon
ITUREA
Abana R.
Damascus
SYRIA
Mt Hermon
PHOENICIA
Tyre
Litani R.
Paneas (Caesarea Philippi)
GAULANITIS
TRACHONITIS
Ptolemais
Main area of Jesus' ministry
GALILEE
Chorazin
Julias
Capernaum
Bethsaida
BATANEA
Genessaret
SEA OF GALILEE
Gergesa
Mt Carmel
Sepphoris
Magdala
Tiberias
AURANITIS
Nazareth
Mt Tabor
Yarmuk R.
DECAPOLIS
Nain
Caesarea Maritima
Scythopolis
Pella
Salim
SAMARIA
Aenon
Jordan R.
Home of Jewish sect: Samaritans
Samaria
Gerasa
Neapolis
Sychar
Mt Gerizim
Jabbok R.
Antipatris
PEREA
Joppa
Phasaelis
Philadelphia
Lydda
Archelais
Jamnia
Jericho
?Emmaus
MEDITERRANEAN SEA
Jerusalem
Bethphage
Julias Livias
Site of Jesus' last week, crucifixion and resurrection
Azotus
Bethany
Qumran
Centre of Essene sect
Bethlehem
Ashkelon
Anthedon Agrippias
JUDEA
Herodium
Machaerus
Hebron
DEAD SEA
Gaza
Arnon R.
Gerar
Besor Brook
IDUMEA
Masada
Areopolis
EASTERN DESERT
NABATEA

Judaism and the Early Church

The Christian faith began in Palestine, regarded by the Jews as their 'promised land'. Jesus, the apostles, and the earliest converts to Christianity were all Jews. After his death, Jesus' followers in Jerusalem formed a community of believers that soon spread, as their message was carried by itinerant preachers and missionaries. At first all believers were Jews, but they were soon joined by Gentiles and were called variously followers of 'the Way', 'Christians', and 'Nazarenes'.

In 62 CE the death of James, leader of the Jerusalem believers, led some to leave the city, weakening its Jewish Christian community. During the First Jewish-Roman War (66–73 CE), Rome destroyed Herod's temple and sacked Jerusalem. The destruction of the temple ended the priesthood and sacrifice system, and proved a lasting disaster for Judaism.

The Christian community probably left Jerusalem just before the siege, taking refuge at Pella, beyond the Jordan, though some believers later returned. Christian communities founded by the apostles near the Mediterranean coast survived, as did those at Capernaum and Rimmon in Galilee, and Cochaba in Gaulanitis.

After the failure of the Jewish Bar Kokhba Revolt (132–35 CE), the Sanhedrin council moved to Jamnia in Galilee. Many Jews were killed, expelled, or sold into slavery after the rebellions against Rome. This, combined with the conversion of pagans, Samaritans, and Jews, gradually resulted in a Christian majority in Palestine. By degrees, Christianity separated from Judaism over several generations and Christian missionaries directed themselves increasingly to Gentiles in the Holy Land and abroad.

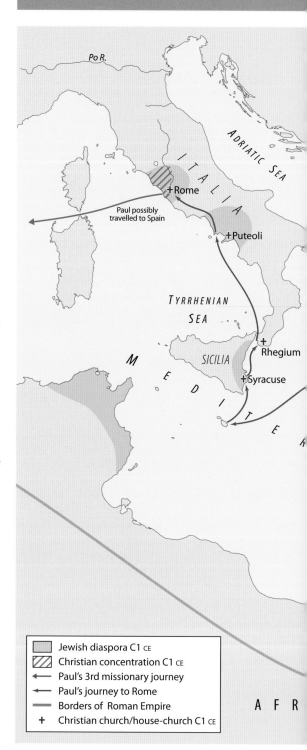

Paul possibly travelled to Spain

▨	Jewish diaspora C1 CE
▨	Christian concentration C1 CE
←	Paul's 3rd missionary journey
←	Paul's journey to Rome
—	Borders of Roman Empire
+	Christian church/house-church C1 CE

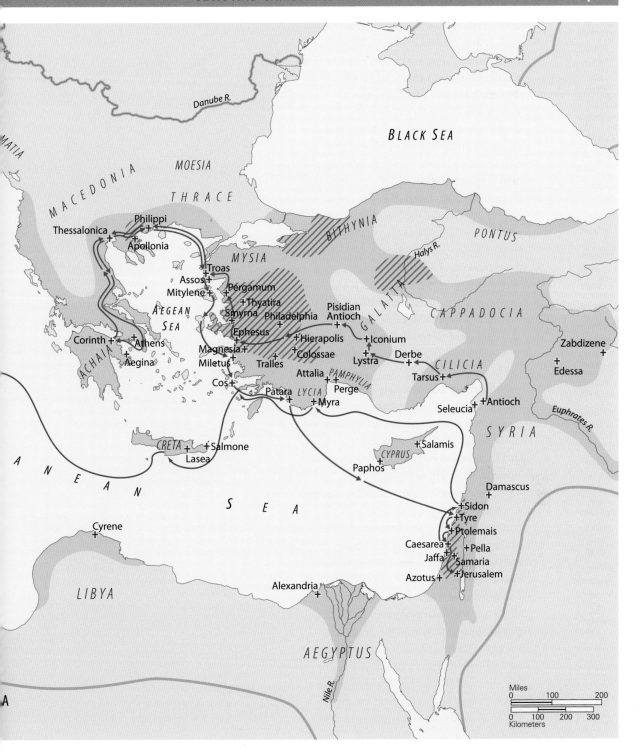

Danube R.

BLACK SEA

DALMATIA

MOESIA

MACEDONIA

THRACE

BITHYNIA

PONTUS

Halys R.

MYSIA

GALATIA

CAPPADOCIA

Thessalonica
Philippi
Apollonia
Troas
Assos
Pergamum
Mitylene
Thyatira
Smyrna
Philadelphia
Pisidian Antioch

AEGEAN SEA

Ephesus
Hierapolis
Iconium
Zabdizene
Corinth
Athens
Magnesia
Colossae
Lystra
Derbe
Edessa
Aegina
ACHAIA
Miletus
Tralles
Attalia
PAMPHYLIA
Tarsus
CILICIA

Cos
Perge
Antioch
Patara
LYCIA
Myra
Seleucia

CRETA
Salmone
Salamis
SYRIA
Lasea
CYPRUS
Euphrates R.

Paphos

Damascus

Sidon
Tyre
Ptolemais
Cyrene
Caesarea
Pella
Jaffa
Samaria
Azotus
Jerusalem

MEDITERRANEAN SEA

LIBYA

Alexandria

AEGYPTUS

Nile R.

Miles
0   100   200

0   100   200   300
Kilometers

The Early Growth of Christianity

Christianity rapidly spread beyond Palestine into the entire Mediterranean area. Within 15 years of the resurrection, a Christian presence was established in Rome itself. Imperial trade routes made possible the rapid traffic of ideas as well as merchandise.

In the eastern Mediterranean, three centres of the Christian church rapidly emerged. The church became a significant presence in its original heartlands, with Jerusalem emerging as a leading centre of thought and activity. Asia Minor, modern-day Turkey, was already an important area of Christian expansion and the destination of several of the apostle Paul's letters. Expansion in this region continued, with the great imperial city of Constantinople, modern Istanbul, a particularly influential centre. Growth also took place to the south, with the city of Alexandria emerging as a stronghold of Christian faith.

With this expansion, new debates opened up. While the New Testament deals with the relationship of Christianity and Judaism, the expansion of Christianity into Greek-speaking regions led to debates about how Christianity related to Greek philosophy.

Christian growth and expansion was not without problems. The 'imperial cult', which regarded worship of the Roman emperor as demonstrating loyalty to the empire, was strong in the eastern Mediterranean, and many Christians were penalized for worshipping only Christ. The spread of Christianity regularly triggered local persecutions: for example the suppression under the Emperor Decius (249–51), which was particularly vicious in North Africa.

Christianity was not officially recognized as a legitimate religion by the Roman state until 313 CE, when Constantine, a recent convert, was joint emperor.

THE SPREAD OF CHRISTIANITY BY 325 CE

NORTH SEA

York
Lincoln

BRITANNIA

London

BELGICA

GE

Rotomagnus
(Rouen)

Rhei

ATLANTIC OCEAN

GALLIA

Lugdunur

Vienne

Bordeaux

Valence

AQUITANIA

Arelate

Narbonne

Mars

Barcelor

HISPANIA

Tarragona

LUSITANIA

Toledo

Carthago
Nova

BAETICA

NUMI

MAURETANIA

Miles
0   100   200   300   400   500

0   100   300   500   700
Kilometers

map 30

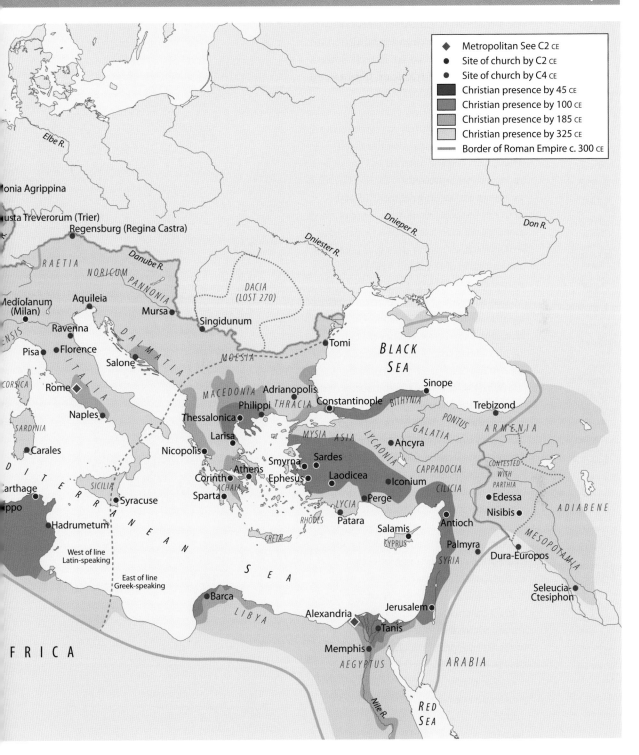

Legend:
- ◆ Metropolitan See C2 CE
- ● Site of church by C2 CE
- ● Site of church by C4 CE
- ▇ Christian presence by 45 CE
- ▇ Christian presence by 100 CE
- ▇ Christian presence by 185 CE
- ▇ Christian presence by 325 CE
- ── Border of Roman Empire c. 300 CE

Elbe R.

onia Agrippina

usta Treverorum (Trier)

Regensburg (Regina Castra)

Dnieper R.

Don R.

Dniester R.

RAETIA

NORICUM

Danube R.

PANNONIA

DACIA
(LOST 270)

Mediolanum
(Milan)

Aquileia

Mursa

Singidunum

Ravenna

DALMATIA

Pisa

Florence

ITALIA

Salone

MOESIA

Tomi

BLACK
SEA

ENSIS

CORSICA

Rome

Naples

SARDINIA

MACEDONIA

Adrianopolis

Philippi

THRACIA

Constantinople

BITHYNIA

Sinope

Trebizond

Thessalonica

Larisa

PONTUS

GALATIA

ARMENIA

MYSIA ASIA

Carales

Nicopolis

Smyrna

Sardes

Ancyra

LYCAONIA

CAPPADOCIA

CONTESTED
WITH
PARTHIA

Carthage

SICILIA

Athens

Corinth

Ephesus

Laodicea

Iconium

CILICIA

Edessa

ADIABENE

ippo

Syracuse

ACHAIA

Sparta

LYCIA

Perge

Nisibis

Hadrumetum

RHODES

Patara

Salamis

Antioch

MESOPOTAMIA

West of line
Latin-speaking

CRETA

CYPRUS

Palmyra

SYRIA

Dura-Europos

East of line
Greek-speaking

MEDITERRANEAN SEA

Barca

LIBYA

Alexandria

Jerusalem

Seleucia-
Ctesiphon

FRICA

Tanis

Memphis

AEGYPTUS

ARABIA

Nile R.

RED
SEA

Christianity Becomes Official

Christianity had become the official religion of the Empire by the end of the 4th century. This new relationship between Christian church and Christian emperor led to turbulent church–state relations in the later Roman Empire and throughout the Middle Ages.

The 4th and 5th centuries were marked by a series of controversies over the identity of Jesus Christ and the doctrine of God. A series of councils strove to resolve these differences and to ensure the unity of the Christian church throughout the Roman Empire. Most important of these councils was Chalcedon (451), which set out the definitive Christian interpretation of the identity of Jesus Christ as 'true God and true man'.

The fall of the Roman Empire, traditionally dated to 476, led to widespread insecurity in the Western church. In the East the church continued to flourish, as the Eastern Empire, based at Constantinople, was largely unaffected by the attacks from northern European invaders that eventually ended Roman power in the West.

The disruptions within the Roman Empire during the 5th century led to a growing rift between the Western and Eastern churches. Increasing tension over political as much as theological issues led eventually to the 'Great Schism' between East and West in 1054.

The removal of Rome as a stabilizing influence gave a significant new role to the church in the West, and particularly to its monasteries. The founding of Benedict of Nursia's first monastery at Monte Cassino around 525 marked the beginning of the monastic movement which was to become so influential in medieval Europe. The pope's role as an increasingly powerful political force also began to emerge during this period.

Border of Roman Empire in 481
Territory under Arian ruler
Area with Monophysite churches
Area of Catholic Christianity
Nestorian church
■ Patriarchal seat
● Church Council or synod
● City with church
← Tribal movements

ITES

FRISIANS
ANGLES
SAXONS

Elbe R.

THURINGIANS

NNI

SLAVS

LOMBARDS

Lauriacum
(Enns)
Danube R.

HUNS

GEPIDS

ALANS

CASPIAN SEA

Mediolanum
(Milan)

Aquileia

OSTROGOTHIC
KINGDOM

Rome
431: Alaric sacks city

Sardica

BLACK SEA

451: 4th Ecumenical Council:
against Monophysites

381: 2nd Ecumenical Council
Constantinople

Chalcedon

Nicaea
325: 1st Ecumenical Council:
against Arians

Ephesus
431: 3rd Ecumenical Council:
against Nestorians

Sebaste

ARMENIAN
CHURCH

Manzikert

Valarshapat
491: Monophysite synod

PERSIAN
EMPIRE

JACOBITE
CHURCH ■ Edessa

Perge Tarsus

Antioch

Nisibis

Euphrates R.

Tigris R.

Carthage

TERRANEAN

NGDOM

SEA

Damascus

Seleucia

Alexandria

COPTIC CHURCH

Jerusalem

Oxyrhyncus

Nile R.

ARABS

RED
SEA

Ptolemais

Ethiopian Church moves towards Monophysites

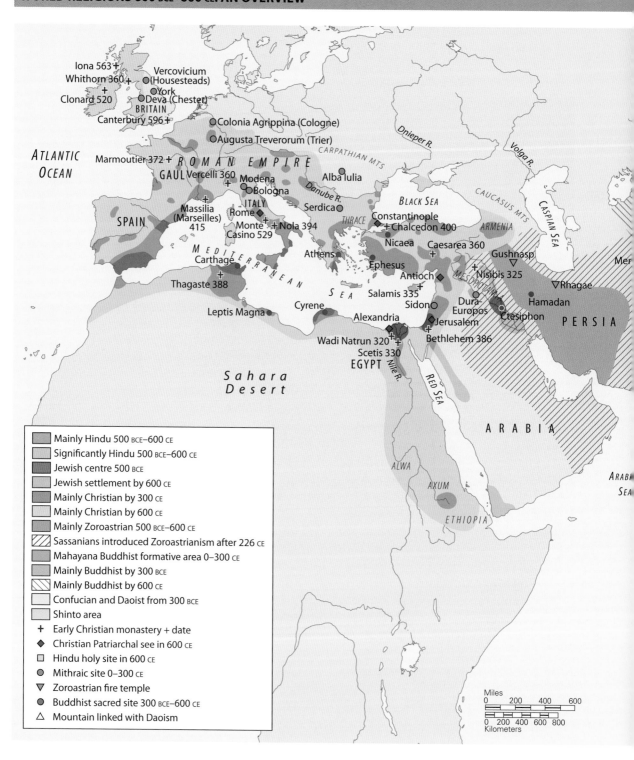

Iona 563 +
Whithorn 360 + ○ Vercovicium (Housesteads)
+ ○ York
Clonard 520 ○ Deva (Chester)
BRITAIN
Canterbury 596 +
○ Colonia Agrippina (Cologne)
○ Augusta Treverorum (Trier)

ATLANTIC OCEAN
Marmoutier 372 + ROMAN EMPIRE
GAUL Vercelli 360
+ ○ Modena
+ ○ Bologna
Massilia (Marseilles) 415
+ Rome ◆ ITALY
Monte + Nola 394
Casino 529
SPAIN
Alba Iulia
Danube R.
Serdica ○
CARPATHIAN MTS
Dnieper R.
Volga R.
BLACK SEA
CAUCASUS MTS
CASPIAN SEA
Constantinople + Chalcedon 400
Nicaea
Caesarea 360
ARMENIA
Gushnasp ▽
Mer
▽ Rhagae
MEDITERRANEAN
Carthage +
Thagaste 388 +
Athens
Ephesus
Antioch ◆
Salamis 335
Sidon ○
Dura-Europos
Nisibis 325 +
MESOPOTAMIA
Hamadan ●
Ctesiphon ◎
PERSIA
SEA
THRACE
Leptis Magna ●
Cyrene
Alexandria ◆
Wadi Natrun 320 +
Scetis 330
EGYPT
Jerusalem ◆
+ Bethlehem 386
Nile R.
RED SEA
ARABIA
Sahara Desert
ALWA
AXUM
ARABIAN SEA
ETHIOPIA

Mainly Hindu 500 BCE–600 CE
Significantly Hindu 500 BCE–600 CE
Jewish centre 500 BCE
Jewish settlement by 600 CE
Mainly Christian by 300 CE
Mainly Christian by 600 CE
Mainly Zoroastrian 500 BCE–600 CE
Sassanians introduced Zoroastrianism after 226 CE
Mahayana Buddhist formative area 0–300 CE
Mainly Buddhist by 300 BCE
Mainly Buddhist by 600 CE
Confucian and Daoist from 300 BCE
Shinto area
+ Early Christian monastery + date
◆ Christian Patriarchal see in 600 CE
□ Hindu holy site in 600 CE
○ Mithraic site 0–300 CE
▽ Zoroastrian fire temple
● Buddhist sacred site 300 BCE–600 CE
△ Mountain linked with Daoism

Miles
0 200 400 600
0 200 400 600 800
Kilometers

map 32

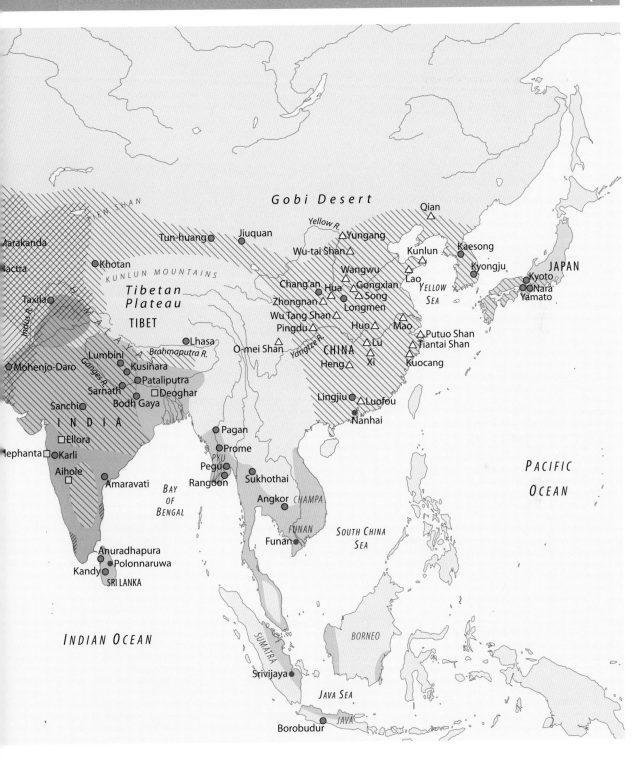

Marakanda
Bactra
Taxila
Mohenjo-Daro
Sanchi
Ellora
Elephanta
Karli
Aihole
Amaravati

TIEN SHAN
KUNLUN MOUNTAINS
Tibetan Plateau
TIBET
Lhasa
Lumbini
Kusinara
Pataliputra
Sarnath
Deoghar
Bodh Gaya

INDIA

HIMALAYA
Indus R.
Ganges R.
Brahmaputra R.

Gobi Desert

Tun-huang
Jiuquan
Yellow R.
Wu-tai Shan
Khotan

Chang'an
Zhongnan
Wu Tang Shan
Pingdu
O-mei Shan
Yangtze R.
CHINA
Heng

Hua
Gongxian
Song
Longmen
Huo
Lu
Xi

Kunlun
Lao
Mao

Qian
Yungang
Wangwu

Kaesong
Kyongju

JAPAN
Kyoto
Nara
Yamato

YELLOW SEA

Putuo Shan
Tiantai Shan
Kuocang

Lingjiu
Luofou
Nanhai

BAY OF BENGAL

Pagan
Prome
PYU
Pegu
Rangoon
Sukhothai
Angkor
CHAMPA
FUNAN
Funan

SOUTH CHINA SEA

PACIFIC OCEAN

Anuradhapura
Polonnaruwa
Kandy
SRI LANKA

INDIAN OCEAN

SUMATRA
Srivijaya
BORNEO
JAVA SEA
JAVA
Borobudur

Christendom in 1050 CE

After Charlemagne (c. 742–814), the first Holy Roman Emperor, who had controlled much of Western Europe, the Western Empire gradually disintegrated into warring principalities.

Between 970 and 1048, 48 famine years reduced many in the West to subsistence. Trade declined, communications collapsed, and travel became perilous. The church was the only institution whose influence extended beyond local rulers, and its leaders and monastic communities strove to maintain a civilized way of life.

Conflict increased between rulers and popes, particularly when a reforming pope such as Leo IX (r. 1049–54) attempted to re-establish respect for his office and defend the church's conduct of its own affairs.

Patriarch Michael Cerularius (r. 1043–58) was spiritual head of an Eastern kingdom riven by intrigue and squeezed between the empire of the Bulgars and the expanding Islamic empire of the Turks. After 1025, Orthodox Christianity suffered serious military setbacks in Asia Minor.

In 1054 a dispute over authority brought differences between East and West to a head. The papacy claimed direct succession from Peter – and thus supreme church authority – claiming support from a document known as the 'Donation of Constantine' (later revealed as a fake). Pope Leo IX excommunicated Patriarch Michael Cerularius; in response, the patriarch anathematized the pope, leading to what is known as the 'Great Schism' between East and West.

Around 866 the first Christian bishop was sent to Kiev from Constantinople by Patriarch Photius I. Soon a Christian community arose among the Kievan nobility. In 988 Prince Vladimir I of Kiev (980–1015) instigated the mass baptism of his people, marking the founding of the Russian Orthodox Church.

THE CHURCH IN 1050

Roman Catholic
Orthodox Greek Rite
Orthodox Slavonic Rite
Orthodox Georgian Rite
Patriarchate of Antioch
Nestorian Christianity
Monophysite Christianity
Muslim rule

map 33

Roman Catholic expansion
Eastern Orthodox expansion
Byzantine Empire
Church of Antioch
Church of Antioch expansion
Patriarchal Seat
Archbishopric (selected)
Major monastery (selected)

Novgorod

BALTIC SEA

Bremen
Elbe R.
Magdeburg
Gniezno
ologne OCorvey
OFulda
Mainz
Prague
hine R.
Lorsch
Danube R.
Gran
xeuil
OReichenau Salzburg
asel OSt Gall
Kalocsa

Dniester R.
Dnieper R.
Volga R.

Bobbio
Ravenna
Split
Capua
érins
Rome
Benevento
Acerenza
Dyrrachium
Monte Cassino
Naples
Bari
Amalfi
Brindisi
Salerno
Otranto
Sta. Severina
Cagliari
Vivarium
Reggio

Preslav

BLACK SEA

Constantinople
Studion

Thessalonica

Neocaesarea

Sebastea

CASPIAN SEA

Etchmiadzin
(Valarshapat)

Iconium

Edessa
Tarsus
Hierapolis
Arbela
Antioch
Salamis
Euphrates R.
Carthage
Damascus
Seleucia

DITERRANEAN SEA

Alexandria

Jerusalem

Nile R.

The European Reformations

Between 1000 and 1500 in Western Europe there was a renewal of church life at every level. The pope's authority to intervene in political disputes reached unprecedented levels. A form of theology known as 'scholasticism' developed, with 13th century writers such as Thomas Aquinas and Duns Scotus achieving great theological sophistication.

The 16th century gave rise to a major upheaval within Western Christianity – the Reformation – that had origins in the Renaissance, with its demand for a return to the original sources of Christianity in the New Testament. Alarmed at what they perceived to be the gap between apostolic and medieval visions of Christianity, individuals such as Martin Luther (1483–1546) and Huldrych Zwingli (1484–1531) pressed for reform. For Luther, how people enter into a right relationship with God – the 'doctrine of justification' – needed radical revision in the light of scripture.

Although the need for reform was widely conceded within the church, such reforms proved hugely controversial. Luther and Zwingli found themselves creating reforming communities outside the mainline church instead of reforming it from within, as they had hoped. By the time of John Calvin (1509–64) and his reformation of Geneva, Protestantism had emerged as a distinct type of Christianity, posing a potent threat to the Catholic Church.

In the late 1540s, the Catholic Church itself began a major process of reformation and renewal, referred to as the Catholic Reformation – previously the 'Counter-Reformation'. Religious orders were reformed, and many of the beliefs and practices reformers had objected to were eliminated. Yet significant differences remained between Protestantism and Catholicism.

REFORMATION EUROPE c. 1570

ICELAND
Not to same scale as main map

Miles
0   100   200
0   100 200 300
Kilometers

NORTH SEA

SCOTLAND
Edinburgh

IRELAND
Dublin

York

ENGLAND
1555–6: Protestant bishops burnt
Oxford
WALES
London

ATLANTIC OCEAN

Rouen
1572–88: St Bartholomew Massacre of Huguenots
Paris
Seine R.
Nantes
Tours
Loire R.
Marmoutier
FRANCE
Bordeaux
BEARN
NAVARRE
Toulous
ARAGON
Barcelona
Zaragoza
Oporto
PORTUGAL
SPAIN
Tagus R.
Lisbon
CASTILE
M
Seville

map 34

NORWAY

Christiania

SWEDEN

Stockholm

Helsinki

LIVONIA

Pskov

Riga

COURLAND

BALTIC
SEA

DENMARK

Copenhagen

Königsberg

PRUSSIA

Vilna

Minsk

RUSSIA

LITHUANIA

Emden

Hamburg

Hanover

Elbe R.

Berlin

Warsaw

Münster
1534:
Anabaptist
uprising

Wittenberg

Rhine R.

Cologne

Leipzig

Dresden

SILESIA

Oder R.

P O L A N D

Krakow

Lvov

russels

SAXONY

Frankfurt

Prague

BOHEMIA

MORAVIA

Dnieper R.

PALATINATE

Nuremberg

heims

WÜRTTEMBERG

Danube R.

Vienna

HUNGARY

Dniester R.

Salzburg

AUSTRIA

Graz

Buda

MOLDAVIA

TRANSYLVANIA

FRANCHE
COMTE

SWISS
CONFEDERATION

Pécs

Geneva

MILAN

Brescia

VENETIAN
REPUBLIC

Trieste

WALLACHIA

yon

SAVOY

Milan

Belgrade

Bucharest

Turin

Venice

Rhône R.

GENOA

Ravenna

Danube R.

Avignon

Genoa

Florence

TUSCANY

Camerino
1528: Capuchin
order founded

Mostar

BLACK SEA

Marseilles

PAPAL
STATES

Sofia

O T T O M A N

Rome
1540: Jesuit
order approved

NAPLES

Cagliari

Naples

E M P I R E

Salonica

Palermo

SICILY

Athens

D I T E R R A N E A N   S E A

Roman Catholic
Orthodox
Lutheran
Calvinist/Reformed/Huguenot
Anglican
Muslim

Anabaptist
Hussite/Bohemian Brethren
Waldensian
Socinian

Holy Roman Empire boundary
1566: Iconoclastic rioting
1572: Rioting after St Bartholomew Massacre
Catholic reform institution

THE EUROPEAN REFORMATIONS   95

South America

In this period Spain remained a major colonial power, whereas Portugal's grip on its colonies was weak. A 'patronage system' continued, giving the monarchs of Spain and Portugal responsibility for Christianizing the indigenous population, establishing dioceses, and appointing clergy in their colonies.

The major religious orders mobilized thousands of priests, leading to the almost total – but superficial – Christianization of Latin America. A minority opposed the political and economic oppression suffered by native populations.

Between 1650 and 1720, in vast uncolonized areas of Paraguay, Jesuit priests gathered Indians into villages called *reductions* in an experiment to Christianize them.

North America

Early 17th century immigrants from Britain were soon joined by Lutherans from Scandinavia, Anabaptists from Germany, Calvinists from Holland, and Catholics from Ireland and Italy.

By the mid-18th century, Virginia boasted around 100 Anglican churches. Georgia, not founded till 1733, quickly established the Anglican Church. At the time of the American Revolution, Anglicanism dominated the South, especially the areas of earliest settlement.

In the colonies of Massachusetts and Connecticut the Congregational Church enjoyed legal favour. The Great Awakening of the 1740s intensified enthusiasm and led some to separate from the official church.

Rhode Island and Providence Plantations allowed religious variety and diversity, as practised by the Baptists and Quakers, while Pennsylvania was a haven for persecuted Quakers and other religious dissenters.

The Dutch Reformed religion thrived in New York and New Jersey, joining in the Great Awakening of the 1740s, like the Scottish and Irish Presbyterians of the Middle Colonies, who had begun to settle in this region early in the 18th century.

The chapel of Nuestra Señora de la Evangelización, Lima Cathedral, Peru.

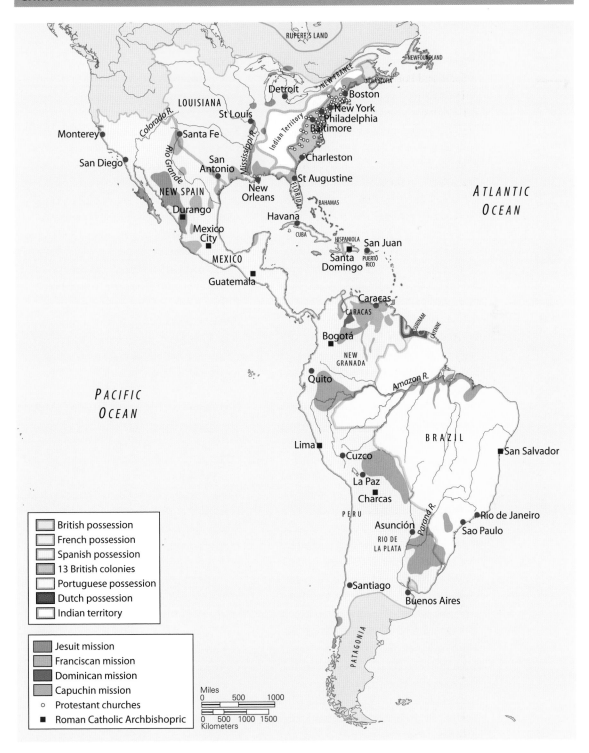

RUPERT'S LAND

NEWFOUNDLAND

NEW FRANCE

NOVA SCOTIA

Detroit

Boston

New York

LOUISIANA

St Louis

Philadelphia

Baltimore

Colorado R.

Monterey

Santa Fe

Indian Territory

Charleston

San Diego

Rio Grande

San Antonio

St Augustine

NEW SPAIN

New Orleans

FLORIDA

ATLANTIC OCEAN

Durango

Mexico City

Havana

BAHAMAS

CUBA

HISPANIOLA

San Juan

MEXICO

Santa Domingo

PUERTO RICO

Guatemala

Caracas

CARACAS

SURINAM

CAYENNE

Bogotá

NEW GRANADA

PACIFIC OCEAN

Quito

Amazon R.

BRAZIL

Lima

San Salvador

Cuzco

La Paz

Charcas

PERU

Parana R.

Río de Janeiro

Asunción

Sao Paulo

RIO DE LA PLATA

Santiago

Buenos Aires

PATAGONIA

British possession
French possession
Spanish possession
13 British colonies
Portuguese possession
Dutch possession
Indian territory

Jesuit mission
Franciscan mission
Dominican mission
Capuchin mission
○ Protestant churches
■ Roman Catholic Archbishopric

Miles
0   500   1000

0 500 1000 1500
Kilometers

An Age of Missions

Beginning in the 18th century, European and American Protestant churches started to send men, and later women, in increasing numbers, to take the Christian message to unreached peoples.

Anglicanism spread outside the British Isles by emigration and missionary effort. The Society for the Propagation of the Gospel in Foreign Parts (1701) and the Society for the Promotion of Christian Knowledge (SPCK, 1698) were both set up to take Anglican Christianity to the British colonies. In North America, missionaries to the Native Americans included Jonathan Edwards (1703–58), the preacher of the Great Awakening.

The pioneering Englishman William Carey (1761–1834) set up the Baptist Missionary Society in 1792. In the Danish trading centre of Serampore, near Calcutta, he printed parts of the Bible in several languages. By 1855, missionaries from the Anglican Church Missionary Society had reached Peshawar. Large numbers of Protestant missionaries from Europe and North America landed in south India, where they encountered – and sometimes clashed with – the Catholic Church founded by Francis Xavier (1506–52) and the Malabar Christian communities of Travancore, believed to date from around the 6th century.

Other societies soon followed the example of Carey's Baptist mission. In 1795 came the London Missionary Society, and in 1797 Dutch Christians formed the Netherlands Missionary Society. In 1799 the Church Missionary Society was founded by Evangelical Anglicans. In 1810 American Evangelicals started the American Board of Commissioners for Foreign Missions, which became a major missionary-sending institution. European Pietists established a missionary training school in Basel, Switzerland in 1815. Often the cross followed the flag: where European powers colonized, missionary societies preached.

Africa

Islam predominated in North Africa, with the exception of Coptic Christians in Egypt and the Ethiopian Church. The first modern missionary activity to achieve success was in the 1830s and 1840s, especially in West Africa.

The first missions to southern Africa were launched in this period from the Cape of Good Hope, where Europeans had long settled. Dr David Livingstone (1813–73), Scottish explorer and missionary, pioneered trails that others followed.

Roman Catholic missions were also active in this period, especially the Holy Ghost Fathers (1848) and White Fathers (1868). Protestant–Catholic rivalry over mission areas intensified, mirroring the political rivalries of the European powers' 'scramble' for African colonies after 1880.

Missions to China and South-East Asia

The first missionary to China in this period was the American Robert Morrison (1782–1834), who arrived in Canton in 1807. However China was not officially open to foreigners until the Treaty of Nanking (1842). Five treaty ports were designated cities for foreign settlement, and British and American missionaries used these as springboards to evangelize China.

Older Roman Catholic missions continued to operate in China, despite persecution. After official toleration was agreed between China and France in 1860, Catholicism was able to expand faster than Protestantism.

After the Taiping Rebellion ended in China in 1864, the British Protestant missionary James Hudson Taylor (1832–1905) set up his China Inland Mission. His mission was one of the few that had much success in persuading Chinese people to convert to Christianity. His example led to the formation of many other missions and to the setting up of the Student Volunteer Movement. Thousands of volunteer missionaries offered their service, and by 1882 Protestant missionaries were resident in all but three of the Chinese provinces.

Following 16th century massacres of Roman Catholic Christians, Japan remained hostile to the West, while South Korea received its first missionary only in 1865.

Latin America

During the 19th century, Protestant missionaries to Latin America came largely from the United States. Protestant values seemed attractive to the liberal middle classes who had won independence for the South American republics. After the ejection of earlier Roman Catholic missions, a shortage of priests had caused a decline in Christian practice.

By the outbreak of World War I, Protestant missions were established in every Latin American republic. However there were only half a million Protestant converts in the entire region – very few compared with the Catholic population.

Oceania

In the 17th century, Spanish Roman Catholics had crossed from the Christianized Philippines to western Micronesia and converted the Marianas Islands. The main Catholic missions in this region were French: in Melanesia, the Congregation of the Sacred Hearts of Jesus and Mary – the 'Pipcus Fathers'; and in Polynesia the Marist Fathers. French Catholics also established themselves in New Caledonia and southern New Guinea, Tahiti, the Marquesas Islands, Mangereva, and Easter Island.

Protestant missionaries progressed generally from east to west, journeying first to Tahiti, then moving on to the Melanesian Islands. London Missionary Society missionaries were the first to reach the Society Islands, before proceeding to Polynesia – Tonga, Western Samoa, and Fiji.

Australia and New Zealand

When Britain decided to set up a penal colony in Australia, an Anglican chaplain, Richard Johnson, went with the first convict ship in 1788. Wesleyans, Presbyterians, and Roman Catholics soon followed. In the 1820s the Anglican church was established, though Irish Catholics and Scots Presbyterians were already numerous.

The first European settlers went to New Zealand in 1805, and the first missionaries nine years later. Anglicans came to form the majority of the population, but with large minorities of Scottish Presbyterians, Roman Catholics, and Methodists.

Missions industry

The 19th century was an age of heroic missionary enterprise, with pioneers such as the English Henry Martyn (1781–1812) in India and Persia; the Americans Adoniram and Ann Judson (1788–1850, 1789–1826) in Burma (Myanmar); the German Johann Krapf (1810–81) in India; the Belgian Father Damien (1840–89) in Hawaii helping those suffering from leprosy; and the Frenchman Father Charles de Foucauld (1858–1916) in North Africa. This was also an age of great mission organizers such as the Irishman H. Grattan Guinness (1835–1910); innovative missionary organizations such as the China Inland Mission and the Mission to Lepers; and great missionary conferences such as the World Missionary Conference in Edinburgh, Scotland (1910), presided over by the Student Volunteer Movement leader, the American John R. Mott (1865–1955).

map 36

Roman Catholic mission active
Protestant mission active

Istanbul

Tehran

Rawalpindi

Jerusalem

Delhi

Karachi

Bombay

Calcutta

Rangoon

Madras

Jaffna

Addis Ababa

Stanleyville

Dar es-Salaam

Blantyre

Durban

Cape Town

Peking

Seoul

Sapporo

Shanghai

Tokyo

Amoy

Hong Kong

Manila

Malacca

Djakarta

Sydney

Melbourne

The Mormons

The Church of Jesus Christ of Latter-Day Saints, or Mormonism as it is often known, was founded in 1830 by Joseph Smith Jr (1805-44) in New York State, USA, as the Church of Christ. In 1834 it became the Church of the Latter-Day Saints, and in 1838 the Church of Jesus Christ of Latter-Day Saints. By 2015 it had some 15.5 million members, more than half of them outside the United States.

Latter-Day Saints describe their church as a 'restoration' movement: God has restored teachings, practices, and organization withdrawn from the earth shortly after the time of Christ as a result of human disobedience.

In 1823, the teenage Joseph Smith Jr found previously hidden metallic records, often called 'the golden plates', that told the history of peoples who migrated to North America from the Holy Land at the time of the Old Testament prophets. Smith translated this text, using special objects found with the plates, and *The Book of Mormon* was published in 1830.

Smith was an inspiring leader and many joined his community, but while in prison in 1844 he was killed by a mob opposed to his religious views, an event Latter-Day Saints viewed as martyrdom. After a brief competition for leadership, Brigham Young (1801–77) triumphed. In 1845 his rival Sidney Rigdon (believed by some to be the author of *The Book of Mormon*) formed his own 'Church of Christ' – also known as the 'Rigdonites' – which survived into the 21st century with a few members as The Church of Jesus Christ (Bickertonite).

After local opposition, Young led the Latter-Day Saints west until they finally arrived in the Great Salt Lake Valley, Utah, in July 1847. Not all followed him, as some believed that leadership should

THE MORMON TRAIL

have passed to Smith's son. This group formed the Reorganized Church of Jesus Christ of Latter-Day Saints in 1860, with its headquarters and temple at Independence, Missouri. This branch is closer to mainstream Christian belief, and in 2001 was renamed the Community of Christ.

In Utah, the original Church of Jesus Christ of Latter-Day Saints prepared for Christ's second coming. Like many Protestants, Latter-Day Saints were Adventist, believing in the return of Jesus, and millenarian, believing he would rule for

map 37

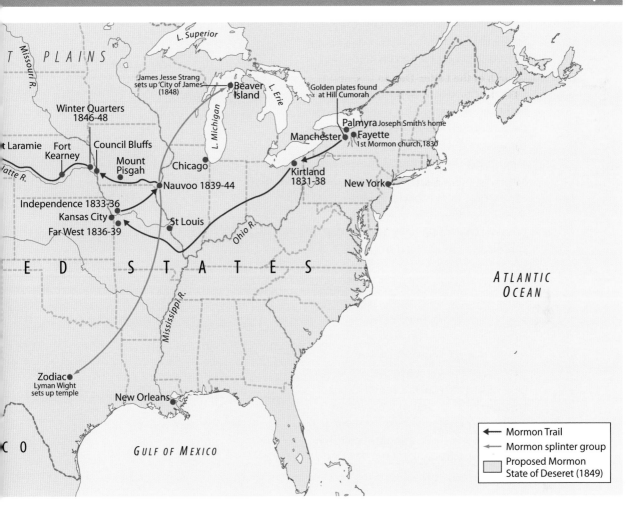

L. Superior

PLAINS

Missouri R.

Winter Quarters 1846-48

James Jesse Strang sets up 'City of James' (1848)

Beaver Island

L. Michigan

L. Erie

Golden plates found at Hill Cumorah

Palmyra   Joseph Smith's home

Manchester   Fayette
1st Mormon church, 1830

t Laramie   Fort Kearney   Council Bluffs

Mount Pisgah

Chicago

latte R.

Nauvoo 1839-44

Kirtland 1831-38

New York

Independence 1833-36

Kansas City

Far West 1836-39

St Louis

Ohio R.

E D   S T A T E S

ATLANTIC OCEAN

Mississippi R.

Zodiac
Lyman Wight sets up temple

New Orleans

C O

GULF OF MEXICO

Legend:
- ← Mormon Trail
- ← Mormon splinter group
- ☐ Proposed Mormon State of Deseret (1849)

1,000 years with his Saints. They thought Christ would appear in the USA.

Smith developed some ideas not found in the Book of Mormon and altered church life in distinctive ways. Many early Saints were alienated by these new doctrines and rituals. Some left, though others regarded these developments as Mormonism's progressive revelation. About a decade after the church was founded, Smith introduced polygamy, which was abandoned at the end of the 19th century.

Today many men and women serve as missionaries for two years before college or marriage. In 2015 the Latter-Day Saints (LDS) church had 74,000 missionaries working worldwide. Since its inception, it claims to have sent more than 1 million members on missions, including such notables as the US presidential candidate Mitt Romney (b. 1947).

Christianity Today

During the 18th century a period of political uncertainty developed in the West, with major implications for the future of Christianity. In France, growing hostility towards the wealth and power of the church hierarchy was an important factor in the French Revolution (1789). Although this revolution did not achieve the permanent removal of Christianity from France, it created an unstable atmosphere. Revolutionary movements across Europe attempted to repeat the successes of their French counterparts, creating serious difficulties for the Catholic Church in many parts of the continent, especially Italy.

Christianity faced new intellectual challenges in the West. During the 1840s, the German philosopher Ludwig Feuerbach (1804–72) argued that the idea of God was merely a projection of the human mind. Karl Marx (1818–83) claimed religion was used by rulers as an instrument of social control. Sigmund Freud (1856–1939) argued it was simply an illusion or 'wish-fulfilment'. By around 1920, many had concluded Christianity was intellectually untenable.

Russia

By this time, other difficulties had arisen, perhaps most importantly the Russian Revolution (1917), which led to the establishment of the world's first avowedly atheist state. The Soviet Union attempted to eliminate religion from public and private life, especially during the 1930s. The Allied defeat of Nazi Germany in World War II led to large areas of Eastern Europe coming under Soviet influence, and the state adoption of anti-religious policies.

The visit to Poland in 1979 of the Polish Pope John Paul II (r. 1978–2005), during which up to one third of the population

CHRISTIANITY WORLDWIDE

- 0–10%
- 11–50%
- 51–70%
- 71–90%
- over 91%

Miles
0   1000   2000

0   1000   2000
Kilometers

met him, together with the formation of the *Solidarnosc* (Solidarity) movement there, helped pave the way for a peaceful transition to democracy and religious freedom in Poland and elsewhere in Eastern Europe. With the fall of the Berlin Wall in 1989, a new openness to religion developed in Russia and the former Soviet spheres of influence, with Christianity – especially Orthodoxy – and Islam experiencing a major renaissance.

map 38

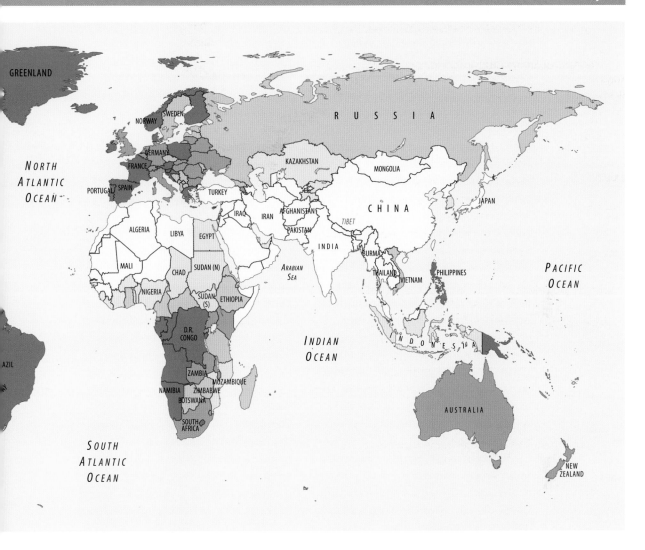

In Russia, the contemporary Orthodox Church often aligns itself with the state and follows a conservative line theologically and socially.

Yet the epicentre of Christianity has moved away from the West.

Worldwide expansion

The 16th century saw the start of a process that has decisively impacted the shaping of Christianity. In addition to the burgeoning missionary movement, an important factor in spreading Christianity globally has been the large-scale emigration from Europe to North America, beginning in the late 16th century.

Today Christianity is primarily a faith of the developing, rather than the developed, world. Although European and American missionaries played a significant role in planting Christianity in regions such as Asia and Africa, these are now largely self-sufficient. The churches of Europe and North

America face the challenges of secularization, while the faith grows rapidly in diverse cultural settings in the non-Western world. In the mid-20th century, as colonial empires were receding, indigenous forms of Christianity displayed considerable growth, demonstrating that the faith had put down roots in local cultures and languages.

The phenomenal growth of Christianity across the southern continents in modern times is unprecedented. Embraced by millions of non-Western believers, the faith is being reshaped through its encounter with the cultures of Latin America, Africa, and Asia. While Western missions played a crucial initial role in communicating the gospel across cultural and linguistic barriers, the key players in the spread of the faith have been local Christians, expressing their new religion in surprising and dynamic ways. Examples include the evangelization of West Africa by repatriated slaves; ordinary Christians adept at sharing their faith and planting new churches; and the ministry of prophetic preachers and evangelists who apply the faith to local situations, resulting in mass conversions.

The centre of gravity of Christianity has shifted and its roots are now firmly planted in non-Western cultures. This shift has revealed contrasts of culture and theology between the different traditions and cultures. For instance, Conservative Anglicans have opposed the ordination of women. Even more divisive between Anglicans in Western and non-Western cultures are attitudes towards gay marriage, and the ministry of gay men and women, both of which are anathema to many in non-Western cultures. Such issues threaten the unity of the Anglican Communion in the early 21st century.

But this shift is also marked by huge church growth in non-Western areas. In South America, the Roman Catholic Church remains strong numerically, and acquired new influence internationally with the papacy of the Argentinian Pope Francis (b. 1936). But Latin America has also seen the extraordinarily rapid growth of indigenous forms of Pentecostal Christianity, with the conversion of more than 40 million people.

Africa

During the 20th century, Africa offered remarkable evidence of Christian growth, and is displacing Europe and North America as the chief Christian heartland. Both the Roman Catholic Church and major Protestant groups are being transformed by these changes, as the number of adherents in Africa dwarfs the parent churches in Europe and North America. Africa has also seen numerous Independent churches flourish – in the 1980s and 1990s especially – as well as many other charismatic and Pentecostal churches.

Asia

The picture is different in Asia. In many countries Christians remain a small minority, in societies shaped by ancient non-Christian religious traditions. Exceptions include South Korea – where growing churches display missionary enthusiasm – Singapore, and the Philippines.

The America-generated 'Prosperity Gospel', offering believers worldly success, has proved attractive in South Korea, where another US model – the 'mega church' – has also blossomed. The small Christian community in Japan has had some gifted theologians and writers. The church in India has initiated attempts to express the gospel in the context of the Hindu-moulded culture.

In China, following the expulsion of Western missions after the Communist revolution, Christianity discarded its image as a foreign import and is now clearly identified as an indigenous religion. Estimates of the number of Christians vary between 30 and 105 million, but there is clear evidence of tenfold growth in the Chinese churches since 1949. This reflects partly the impact of the Home Church Movement, the number of whose congregations increased from around 50,000 in 1970 to 400,000 in 1995.

World Christianity

Until recently it was assumed that the churches of Europe and North America could be transplanted to other continents, complete with their theology and practice. This assumption rested on the belief that Western Christianity was a culture-free expression of the faith and possessed absolute status. With the emergence of non-Western churches, such assumptions have had to be abandoned. Theology can take unexpected directions in cultures relatively unaffected by Western modernity.

The non-Western churches are mainly churches of the poor, in a world moulded by economic globalization. Old one-way Christian missionary approaches – from the West to the rest – have been supplanted

Higher Vision Church, Valencia, California, U.S.A.

by more complex patterns, where mission is from everywhere to everywhere. Recent massive migrations from southern continents into Europe and North America are resulting in the appearance of 'Southern' forms of Christianity, such as prophetic and charismatic shop front churches, in the great urban centres of the Western world, where they often form the largest and most dynamic Christian communities.

Part 6

Islam

Muhammad

Islam began, not among nomads, but among city-dwellers engaged in commercial enterprises. Towards the end of the 6th century CE, the merchants of Mecca gained a monopoly of the trade between the Indian Ocean and the Mediterranean that passed along the west coast of Arabia by camel caravan. Mecca had a sanctuary, the *Ka'ba*, which was an ancient pilgrimage centre, and the area around it was regarded as sacred. However the wealth that came to Mecca led to social tensions, especially among the younger males.

Muhammad was born in Mecca around the year 570 CE. In about 610 he came to believe he was receiving messages from God which he was to pass on to his fellow citizens. Revealed over 23 years, these messages were later collected and form the *Qur'an*. They claimed that God was One (*Allah*), and that he was merciful and all-powerful. *Allah* expected people to use their wealth generously. On the Last Day, he would judge people according to their acts and assign them to heaven or hell. In these revelations, Muhammad himself was spoken of, sometimes simply as a warner, telling of God's punishment for sinners, and sometimes as a prophet, or messenger of God. Muhammad believed these revelations were the words of God, conveyed to him by an angel.

Muhammad gained a number of followers, who met frequently and joined him in worshipping God. But Meccan merchants were annoyed by criticism of their practices. The merchants spoke of old pagan gods; Muhammad's messages insisted there is only one God.

Emigration to Medina

Muhammad's followers began to be persecuted by opponents – often their own relatives – and eventually it became impossible for Muhammad to continue in Mecca. In 622 CE Muhammad and about 70 men emigrated with their families to nearby Medina, a fertile oasis. This migration, the *Hijrah*, marks the beginning of the Islamic era. The inhabitants of Medina divided into two opposing groups, with the majority accepting Muhammad as prophet and agreeing to form a federation with the emigrants from Mecca.

In Medina the religion of Islam took shape. The main ritual forms – modelled on Muhammad's example – were: worship (or prayer), almsgiving, fasting for the month of Ramadan, and pilgrimage to Mecca, including ceremonies at sites nearby.

At first, Muhammad had no special political powers at Medina beyond being leader of the emigrants from Mecca. However after a year or two his followers – now called 'Muslims' – became involved in hostilities with the pagan Meccans. By 630, Muhammad had become strong enough to capture Mecca. He treated his enemies generously, and won most of them over to become Muslims. Many other tribes across Arabia now also joined his federation and became Muslims. Muhammad's authority as head of state was unquestioned because of his success.

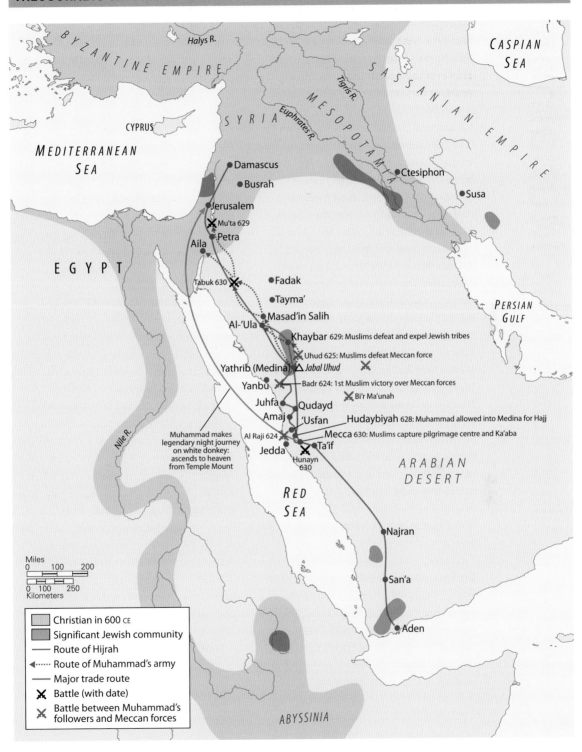

CASPIAN
SEA

Halys R.

BYZANTINE EMPIRE

Tigris R.

SASSANIAN EMPIRE

MESOPOTAMIA

SYRIA

Euphrates R.

CYPRUS

●Ctesiphon

●Susa

MEDITERRANEAN
SEA

●Damascus

●Busrah

●Jerusalem

✖ Mu'ta 629

Petra●

Aila●

EGYPT

Tabuk 630 ✖

●Fadak

●Tayma'

●Masad'in Salih

Al-'Ula●

PERSIAN
GULF

Khaybar 629: Muslims defeat and expel Jewish tribes

✖ Uhud 625: Muslims defeat Meccan force

Yathrib (Medina)● △ *Jabal Uhud*

✖

Yanbu●

Badr 624: 1st Muslim victory over Meccan forces

Juhfa●

✖ Bi'r Ma'unah

Qudayd●

Amaj●

'Usfan●

Hudaybiyah 628: Muhammad allowed into Medina for Hajj

Al Raji 624

Nile R.

Muhammad makes
legendary night journey
on white donkey:
ascends to heaven
from Temple Mount

Mecca 630: Muslims capture pilgrimage centre and Ka'aba

Jedda●

●Ta'if

Hunayn
630

ARABIAN
DESERT

RED
SEA

●Najran

Miles
0   100   200

0 100 250
Kilometers

●San'a

●Aden

	Christian in 600 CE
	Significant Jewish community
——	Route of Hijrah
◄····	Route of Muhammad's army
——	Major trade route
✖	Battle (with date)
✖	Battle between Muhammad's followers and Meccan forces

ABYSSINIA

The Early Growth of Islam

Muhammad died in 632, leaving a religion and a state. His first successor was Abu Bakr (c. 573–634), the 'caliph' (*khalifa*) – 'successor' or 'deputy' of Muhammad. Muhammad and the first caliphs organized successful raiding expeditions towards Syria and Iraq to obtain booty.

There was a temporary power vacuum in the region because the two great powers – the Byzantine and Persian Empires – had been almost constantly at war for 50 years and were exhausted. In a few decisive battles the Muslims overcame any opposition that these empires presented. Instead of returning to Medina, they then ventured further afield.

Within 12 years of Muhammad's death, Muslim armies had occupied Egypt, Syria, and Iraq, and were advancing westwards into Libya and eastwards into what is now Iran. The Byzantine and Persian provincial governors fled and the Muslims made treaties with local inhabitants, calling them 'protected minorities'. These groups organized their own internal affairs, but paid tribute or tax to the Muslim governor. The status of protected minority was open only to 'people of the book', who believed in one God and possessed a written scripture, such as Jews and Christians.

The expansion of Islam

Apart from some periods of internal strife, Muslim expansion continued for a century. To the west, Muslims occupied North Africa as far as the Atlantic Ocean, crossed into Spain, briefly holding the region around Narbonne, southern France. In 732, at the Battle of Tours in central France, a Muslim raid was defeated by a French army. The Muslims also raided as far as Constantinople (modern Istanbul), but failed to occupy any of Asia Minor (Turkey). After occupying Persia and Afghanistan, they penetrated

central Asia and crossed the Indus river. Until 750, this entire area remained a single state, ruled by caliphs of the Ummayad dynasty.

Most of the inhabitants of these regions were not immediately converted to Islam, but became protected minorities. The military expeditions, though described as 'holy wars' (*jihads*), were raids for booty, not to make converts.

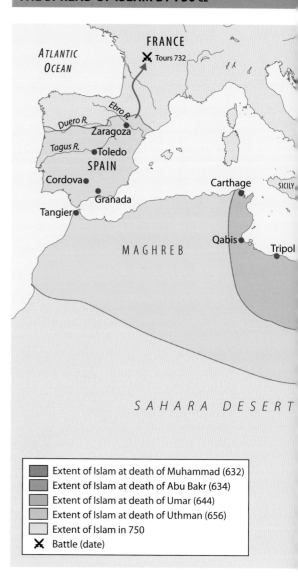

THE SPREAD OF ISLAM BY 750 CE

- Extent of Islam at death of Muhammad (632)
- Extent of Islam at death of Abu Bakr (634)
- Extent of Islam at death of Umar (644)
- Extent of Islam at death of Uthman (656)
- Extent of Islam in 750
- ✗ Battle (date)

map 40

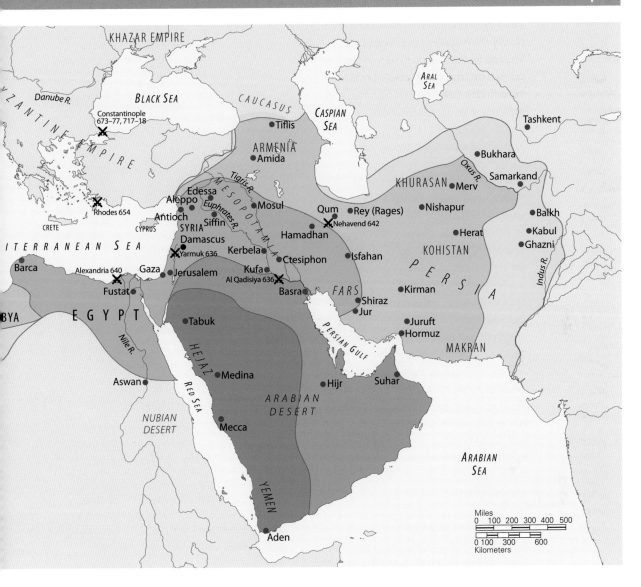

Protected minorities were on the whole well treated. However members of these minorities felt themselves to be second-class citizens, and over the centuries there was a steady flow of converts to Islam. In this way Islam became the dominant religion in lands that were previously the home of Christianity. By the 7th century, Zoroastrianism, the official religion of the Persian Empire, was in decline, and conversion to Islam there was rapid and extensive.

In 750 the Ummayad dynasty of caliphs, based in Damascus, ended, and for the next 500 years, the 'Abbasid dynasty ruled from Baghdad. While the Ummayad period was one of growth, the first centuries of 'Abbasid rule were marked by consolidation.

Islam in the Subcontinent

Islam entered India via two main routes: from the south, where Arab traders had set up colonies along the south-west coast of India in pre-Islamic times, and from the north, where Islam arrived via Central Asia through military conquest. Sind in the north was crucial for the diffusion of Islam, which spread from there to Punjab and Gujarat.

From the 11th century onwards, Muslim penetration was more sustained. A new Turkish 'Ghaznavid' dynasty under Sultan Mahmud (971–1030) started to expand from Ghazni. Hindu rulers from Delhi, Kalinjar, Ajmer, and other cities formed a confederacy to oppose him, but were defeated at the battle of Waihind (1008). Mahmud carried out several campaigns, culminating in the capture of Somnath, but annexed only Punjab.

Masjid Sabz, or Green Mosque, Balkh, Afghanistan.

After the Ghaznavids, other dynasties took Islam into new areas. By 1212, the Ghurid dynasty controlled most of the former Ghaznavid territories and had expanded as far east as Bengal. Later the Afghan Khaljis defended this territory against repeated Mongol raids and, under the great sultan Alauddin Khilji (r. 1296–1316), reached as far south as Madurai.

The Turco-Indian Tughluqids expanded to the south and east, but the vast empire began to disintegrate with the rise of independent Muslim principalities.

The subcontinent was reunified during the 17th century under the Mughal emperors. However, by the 1770s the Mughal Empire (1526–1858) had shrunk to a small province around Delhi. Its legacy re-emerged in 1947 when, as the British withdrew from India, the newly-created Muslim state of Pakistan re-affirmed its links with Persia and the Middle East.

Muslim rulers of India generally practised religious tolerance, since mass conversion of the huge population of Hindus was impossible. Widespread conversions took place only in the Punjab and Bengal. Hindus and Muslims lived together, sometimes harmoniously, sometimes not. Although Islam was often strongly supported by the state, the rapid spread of Islam was mainly due to the missionary activity of Sufi orders.

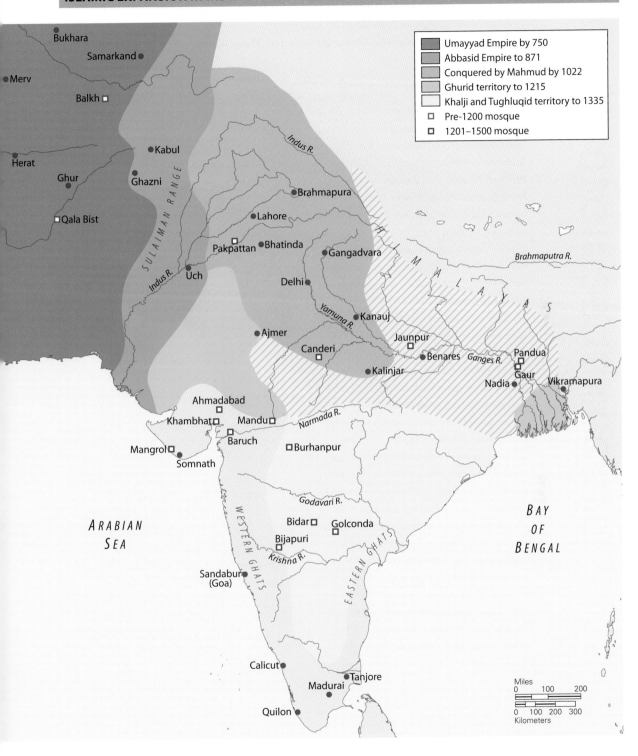

Bukhara

Samarkand

Merv

Balkh

Kabul

Herat

Ghur

Ghazni

Qala Bist

SULAIMAN RANGE

Indus R.

Brahmapura

Lahore

Pakpattan

Bhatinda

Uch

Gangadvara

Delhi

Yamuna R.

Kanauj

Ajmer

Canderi

Jaunpur

Benares

Ganges R.

Pandua

Kalinjar

Gaur

Nadia

Vikramapura

Ahmadabad

Khambhat

Mandu

Narmada R.

Baruch

Mangrol

Burhanpur

Somnath

HIMALAYAS

Brahmaputra R.

ARABIAN
SEA

Godavari R.

Bidar

Golconda

Bijapuri

Krishna R.

WESTERN GHATS

EASTERN GHATS

BAY
OF
BENGAL

Sandabur
(Goa)

Calicut

Tanjore

Madurai

Quilon

	Umayyad Empire by 750
	Abbasid Empire to 871
	Conquered by Mahmud by 1022
	Ghurid territory to 1215
	Khalji and Tughluqid territory to 1335
☐	Pre-1200 mosque
☐	1201–1500 mosque

Miles
0   100   200

0   100   200   300
Kilometers

Islam in South-east Asia

In South-east Asia, the introduction of Islam is linked to trade, which was controlled by the Arabs from the 12th to 15th centuries. After this, the Portuguese commenced global trading.

From the 14th century, local rulers in South-East Asia converted to Islam. Within two centuries almost the entire region had been Islamized. By the mid-15th century Malacca had become the chief trading-centre for South-east Asia and main centre for the spread of Islam, which came to be identified with the state and its main language, Malay.

The embracing of Islam by the rulers of Malacca encouraged the emergence of similar sultanates elsewhere on the Malay Peninsula and farther afield in Jolo, Ternate, and Tidore.

However there is also evidence of conversions to Islam in Sumatra and elsewhere earlier than 1400 CE. A fragment of inscription from the east coast of the Malay Peninsula – the 'Trengganu Stone' – appears to show a ruler pronouncing the primacy of Islamic law, and has been dated to between 1302 and 1387.

Mass conversion in this area was the result of the missionary activities by Sufi orders; political opportunism and obedience to the Muslim sultans; old and repeated contact with Muslim traders; and, after the arrival of Christian missionaries with the Portuguese, a revival of Islamic proselytism.

Today, Islam is the most widely practised religion in this region. It is the official religion of Malaysia and Brunei, and its adherents form a majority of the population in both those countries as well as of Indonesia.

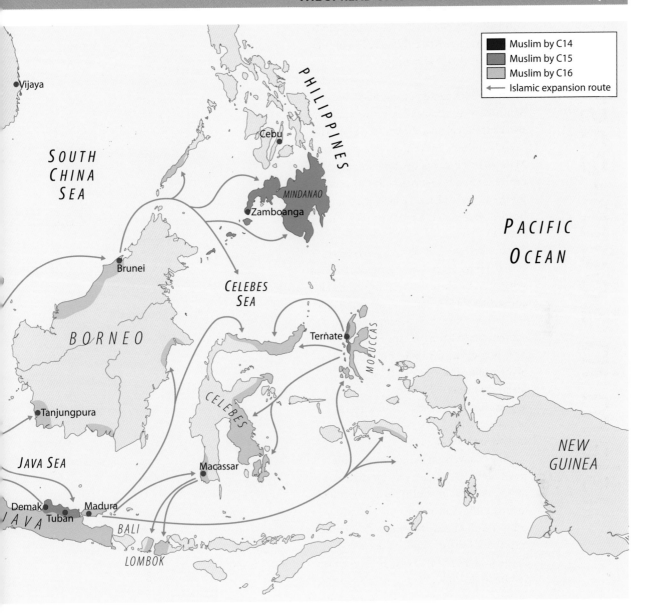

■	Muslim by C14
■	Muslim by C15
■	Muslim by C16
←	Islamic expansion route

Vijaya

SOUTH
CHINA
SEA

PHILIPPINES

Cebu

MINDANAO
Zamboanga

PACIFIC
OCEAN

Brunei

CELEBES
SEA

BORNEO

Ternate

MOLUCCAS

CELEBES

Tanjungpura

NEW
GUINEA

JAVA SEA

Macassar

Demak
Tuban
Madura

JAVA

BALI

LOMBOK

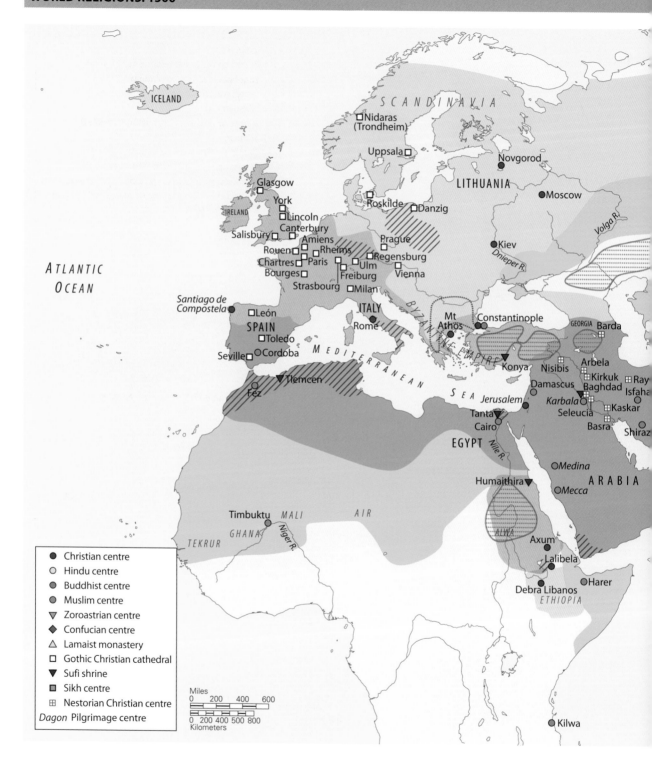

ICELAND

SCANDINAVIA

□ Nidaras
(Trondheim)

Uppsala □

● Novgorod

LITHUANIA

● Moscow

Volga R.

□ Glasgow

□ York

IRELAND

□ Lincoln

□ Canterbury

Salisbury □

□ Roskilde

□ Danzig

● Kiev

Dnieper R.

□ Amiens

Rouen □ □ Rheims

Chartres □ □ Paris

Bourges □

□ Prague

□ Regensburg

□ Ulm

Freiburg □

□ Vienna

Strasbourg □ □ Milan

ATLANTIC
OCEAN

Santiago de
Compostela ●

□ León

ITALY

□ Rome

*Mt
Athos* ●

● Constantinople

BYZANTINE EMPIRE

GEORGIA ● Barda

SPAIN

□ Toledo

Seville □ ○ Cordoba

MEDITERRANEAN SEA

▼ Konya

Nisibis ⊞

Arbela ⊞

⊞ Kirkuk ○ Ray

Damascus ● ⊞ Baghdad ● Isfaha

▼ Tlemcen

Fez ▼

Jerusalem ●

Karbala ○ ▼

⊞ Kaskar

Seleucia ⊞

Basra ⊞

● Shiraz

Tanta ▼

Cairo ▼

EGYPT

Nile R.

○ *Medina*

○ *Mecca*

A R A B I A

Humaithira ▼

Timbuktu ● *MALI*

AIR

GHANA

TEKRUR

Niger R.

ALWA

● Axum

● Lalibela

Debra Libanos ●

● Harer

ETHIOPIA

● Kilwa

● Christian centre
○ Hindu centre
◐ Buddhist centre
● Muslim centre
▼ Zoroastrian centre
◆ Confucian centre
△ Lamaist monastery
□ Gothic Christian cathedral
▼ Sufi shrine
■ Sikh centre
⊞ Nestorian Christian centre

Dagon Pilgrimage centre

Miles
0   200   400   600

0 200 400 500 800
Kilometers

map 43

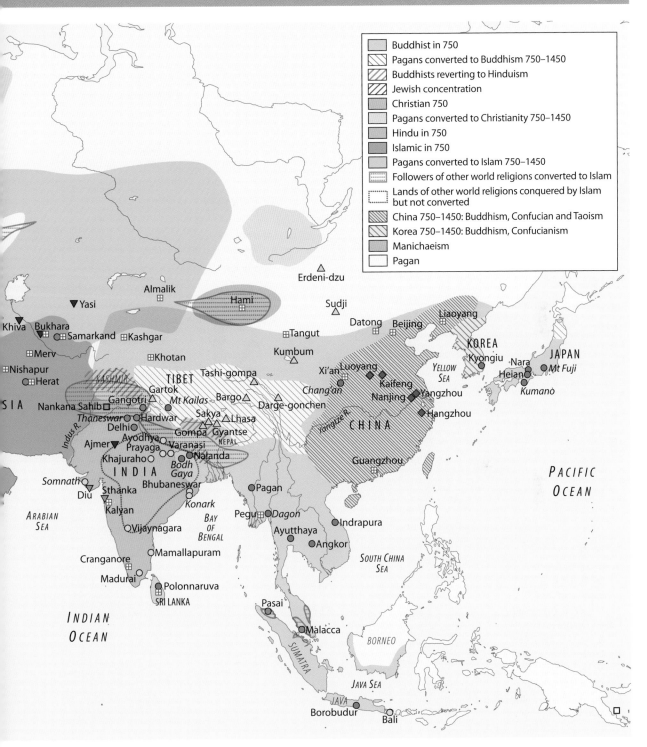

Legend:
- Buddhist in 750
- Pagans converted to Buddhism 750–1450
- Buddhists reverting to Hinduism
- Jewish concentration
- Christian 750
- Pagans converted to Christianity 750–1450
- Hindu in 750
- Islamic in 750
- Pagans converted to Islam 750–1450
- Followers of other world religions converted to Islam
- Lands of other world religions conquered by Islam but not converted
- China 750–1450: Buddhism, Confucian and Taoism
- Korea 750–1450: Buddhism, Confucianism
- Manichaeism
- Pagan

Erdeni-dzu

Almalik
Hami
Sudji
Yasi
Datong   Beijing   Liaoyang
Khiva Bukhara
Samarkand Kashgar   Tangut
Merv   Kumbum   KOREA
Nishapur   Khotan   Kyongiu
Herat   TIBET   Tashi-gompa   Xi'an Luoyang   Nara Mt Fuji
Gartok   Chang'an   Kaifeng   Heian
NASHMIR   Mt Kailas   Bargo   Kumanò
Nankana Sahib   Gangotri   Darge-gonchen   Nanjing   Yangzhou
Thaneswar Hardwar   Sakya Lhasa   CHINA   Hangzhou
Delhi   Gompa Gyantse   YELLOW SEA
Ajmer   Ayodhya   NEPAL
Prayaga   Varanasi
Khajuraho   Nalanda   Guangzhou
INDIA   Bodh Gaya
Somnath   Bhubaneswar   PACIFIC OCEAN
Diu Sthanka   Konark
Kalyan   Pagan
ARABIAN SEA   Pegu Dagon   Indrapura
BAY OF BENGAL   Ayutthaya
Vijaynagara   Angkor
Mamallapuram   SOUTH CHINA SEA
Cranganore   JAPAN
Madurai   Polonnaruva   BORNEO
SRI LANKA
INDIAN OCEAN   Pasai
SUMATRA   Malacca
JAVA SEA
JAVA   Borobudur   Bali

Yangtze R.
Indus R.

ISLAM IN SOUTH-EAST ASIA   119

Islam and Africa

The Muslim penetration of Africa involved conquest, trade, migration, and missionary activities. During the 7th and 8th centuries CE, Arab military conquests of Egypt and much of North Africa were gradually followed by the conversion of much of the Berber population to Islam.

From the 11th to the 14th century, Islam spread across the Sahara into West Africa and up the Nile river into the Sudan, travelling along the trade routes connecting West Africa with North Africa. From an area between Morocco and Senegal, new Berber converts – later known as the 'Almoravids' – conquered Morocco, crossed to Spain, and fought the Christian rulers, ruling Iberia for almost a century (1086–1147).

In East Africa, Islam was carried down the coast by sea-going Arabs, some of whom settled and built up coastal cities such as Sofala and Kilwa, major ports in the gold trade.

Between the 16th and 18th centuries, Muslim scholars, Sufis, and Muslim traders helped form states ruled by Muslim princes, such as the Sultanate of Funj and Kingdom of Kanem-Bornu, which became a great trading and military power in the late 16th century. The greatest state of Saharan Africa was the Songhai Empire, Muslim since 1493, which controlled the trans-Saharan gold trade until the early 17th century.

During this period too, Muslim Malays and Javanese emigrated from the Dutch East Indies to South Africa, especially the Cape Town region, becoming the first Muslims to settle in South Africa.

From the 18th century some Sufi orders, especially the Qadiriyah and the Tijaniyah, led by militants who declared a *jihad*, seized local political control, aiming to set up 'pure' Islamic governments. Examples include the Sokoto state in Hausaland, founded in 1804 by Uthman Dan Fodio, and the Mahdist state of Eastern Sudan (1882–96), the result of an Islamic renewal movement fighting against colonists.

In recent times there has been a revival of Islam in Africa, partly in response to secularism. Islamic missionary activities, often using local missionaries, flourish. The close relation of Islam with some African beliefs, for example the belief in good and bad spirits, associated with the Muslim belief in *jinns*, is another reason for Islam's successful expansion.

Recent waves of immigration from South and South-east Asia to East Africa and, as a result of Ugandan ruler Idi Amin's (1971–9) persecution of Asians, from East Africa to Southern Africa, have added to the variety of Islam in the continent. Among them are Sunnis of the Shafi'i legal school, Shi'ites, and Pakistani Ahmadis.

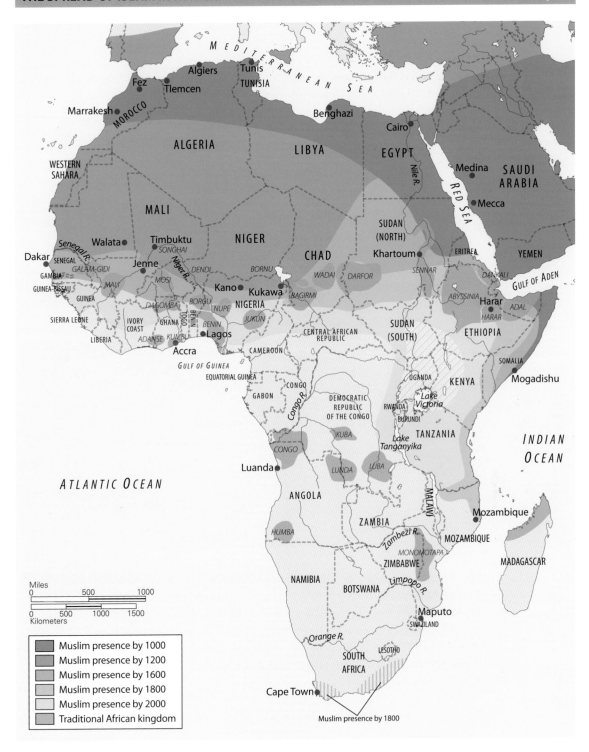

Miles
0   500   1000

0   500   1000   1500
Kilometers

- Muslim presence by 1000
- Muslim presence by 1200
- Muslim presence by 1600
- Muslim presence by 1800
- Muslim presence by 2000
- Traditional African kingdom

Muslim presence by 1800

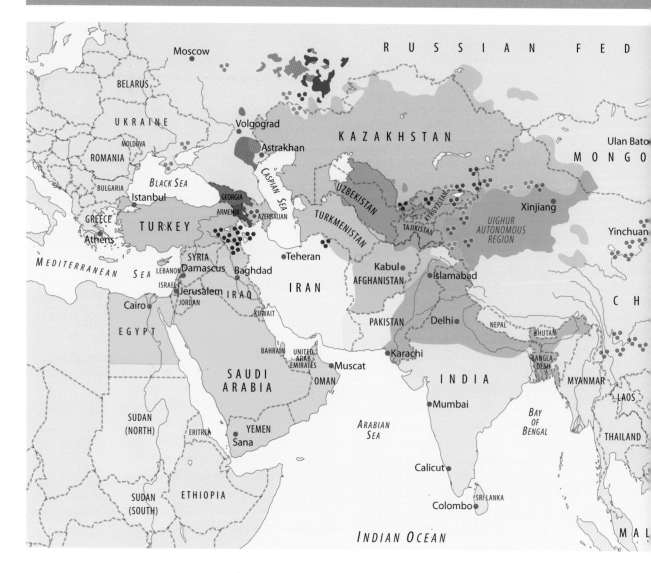

Since the Middle Ages the lands between the Black Sea, the Caspian Sea, and China have been linked by trade routes – the River Volga and the Silk Road to China. Islam expanded along these routes, sometimes by conquest, but mainly through trade and Sufi missionaries. In modern times, Muslims in this area have been linked politically, as most countries were under Soviet or Chinese communist rule. Since the breakdown of the Soviet Union in 1991, religious activities have revived and new Muslim countries have emerged.

Between the 7th and the 9th centuries, Islam spread by conquest to Central Asia and the

Caucasus, and later spread peacefully through commerce. By the 12th century Islam stretched

map 45

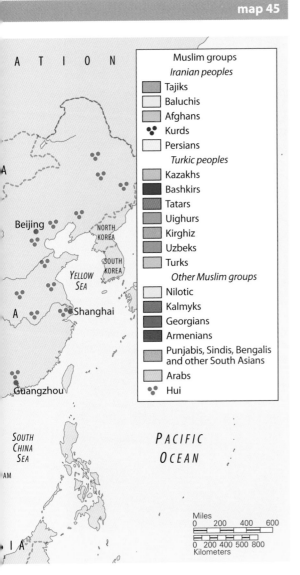

Muslim groups

Iranian peoples
- Tajiks
- Baluchis
- Afghans
- Kurds
- Persians

Turkic peoples
- Kazakhs
- Bashkirs
- Tatars
- Uighurs
- Kirghiz
- Uzbeks
- Turks

Other Muslim groups
- Nilotic
- Kalmyks
- Georgians
- Armenians
- Punjabis, Sindis, Bengalis and other South Asians
- Arabs
- Hui

A T I O N

A

NORTH KOREA

Beijing

SOUTH KOREA

YELLOW SEA

A

Shanghai

Guangzhou

SOUTH CHINA SEA

AM

PACIFIC OCEAN

I A

Miles
0   200   400   600

0   200 400 500 800
Kilometers

imam Shamil (r. 1834–59) and Uzun Haji (d. 1920), rebelled against the Russians in the northern Caucasus.

The Russian Revolution of 1917 resulted in an anti-religious policy, and overt Muslim religious rituals and practices were restricted, mosques destroyed, and Muslim schools and colleges proscribed. Anti-religious campaigns intensified in the 1950s and 1960s. During the late 1980s, the Russian leader Mikhail Gorbachev's (b. 1931) policy of *glasnost* (openness) aimed at permitting some freedom of thought and belief, and marked the beginning of Muslim political revival. By 1991, the Muslim states of Kazakhstan, Uzbekistan, Tajikistan, Kyrgyzstan, Turkmenistan, and Azerbaijan had emerged as independent republics.

Most Muslims in southern Russia, Central Asia, and the Caucasus are Sunnis, following the Hanafi school of law. Most Daghestanis, Chechno-Ingush and some Kurds follow the Shafi'i school. There are Shi'a Muslims among the Tajiks, the Uzbeks, the Baluchis, the Azeris, and Tats. There are also Isma'ilis, especially in the Pamirs in Central Asia, and some Baha'is in southern Russia, Azerbaijan, and Turkmenistan. Sufi orders are particularly important in Central Asia and the northern Caucasus.

Islam in China

The exact number of Chinese Muslims is unknown, partly because of the Communist government's repressive policy toward Islam. The two most significant groups are the Hui, who speak languages such as Tibetan and Mongolian, and the Uighur who speak a Turkic language.

The first Muslim settlers in China were merchants who arrived from the 7th century onward. Those coming by sea settled in the south-eastern coastal region, around modern-day Guangzhou (Canton).

from the Urals to modern Kazakhstan, Kyrgyzstan, and Xinjiang. By the 16th century it extended as far as the Russian steppes, north of the Black Sea and Caspian Sea.

As the Russian Empire expanded, from the 14th to the 19th century, it incorporated Muslim territories. Apart from Catherine the Great (r. 1762–96), Russian rulers denied Muslims religious rights. Sufi-inspired *jihad* movements, such as those led by Naqshbandi

Islam in Modern Asia

Decorated mihrab of the Kalon mosque, Bukhara, Uzbekistan.

Those arriving via the Silk Road reached Xinjiang; some headed to modern-day Xi'an (Chang'an), often stopping at Lanzhou. These early settlers included Arabs, Persians, and Mongols.

There were further migrations to China during the Mongol Yuan dynasty (1279–1368), when Muslims traded with Central Asia. The first Muslim community in Yunnan province can be dated to this period. The Ming dynasty (1368–1644) was generally tolerant towards Muslims and encouraged assimilation. Sufism entered China as a major force late in the 17th century, arriving from Central Asia along the main trade routes.

When the Qing dynasty (1644–1911) expanded into Central Asia, Muslims started to rebel, asserting their identity and rejecting any compromises with local religions. The Qing quashed major 19th-century Muslim rebellions in Yunnan and north-west China. Muslims of the north-west were granted autonomy only after the fall of the Qing dynasty.

The policy of the Chinese People's Republic towards Muslims has oscillated between tolerance and radicalism. During the Cultural Revolution (1966–76), Muslims in Yunnan were persecuted under both anti-ethnic and anti-religious policies.

Recent Islamic militancy, especially in the north-west, has prompted an increased Chinese military presence. This region has become commercially and strategically important for China because of its mineral resources and its trade links with Central Asia, the Middle East, and the West.

Uighur men outside the Id Kah Mosque at the end of Ramadan. Kashgar, Xinjiang province, western China.

Islam in the Modern World

By the end of World War I, the Muslim empires had been dismembered, and European colonial powers occupied or directly influenced the Muslim world. 'Modernity' was regarded as a transformation originating in Europe and North America. Muslims experienced Europe's power not as secular, but as Christian. While Muslims welcomed the material benefits of science and technology, they remained ambivalent to modern values, such as democracy, and hostile to missionary propaganda that contradicted the core of their faith. In countries such as India, Algeria, and Palestine, the retreat from colonial rule left much suffering and bitterness.

Two major Sunni modernist reformers, the Indian Sayyid Ahmad Khan (1817–98) and the Egyptian Muhammad 'Abduh (1845–1905), held that every Muslim could search scripture's meaning for himself or herself.

More radical reformers aimed to Islamicize modernity, rather than modernize Islam. Two key radicals helped shape movements that are sometimes called 'fundamentalist' or 'Islamist': the Indian/Pakistani Abu al-Ala Maududi (1903–79) and the Egyptian Sayyid Qutb (1906–66). Both men believed Muslims should conduct their entire lives according to God's law, and provided an incisive critique of secular Western societies. A similar impulse moved Ayatollah Khomeini's revolution in Iran (1979).

In the USA, some of the Black Power movements drew on Islamic themes. The Nation of Islam (NOI) was originally a black supremacist organization, established in the 1930s and later led by Elijah Muhammad (Elijah Poole, 1897–1975).

White people's interest in Islam tends to focus on Sufism, originally introduced to the

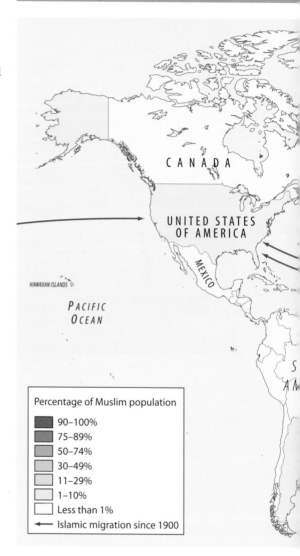

ISLAM WORLDWIDE TODAY

Percentage of Muslim population

- 90–100%
- 75–89%
- 50–74%
- 30–49%
- 11–29%
- 1–10%
- Less than 1%
- ← Islamic migration since 1900

USA in 1910 by Inayat Khan (1882–1927), and made popular by the writings of Idries Shah (1924–96). In the West, small numbers of white converts, particularly in areas of high Muslim immigration, have converted to Islam, having found other various aspects of the religion appealing.

The majority of Muslims in Western society live peacefully, often with workplace adaptations to meet their religious

map 46

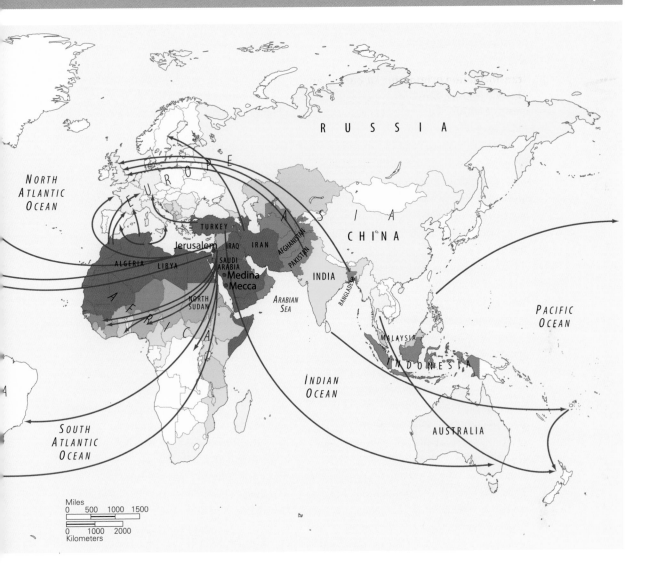

requirements at times such as the Ramadan fast. However for some in the West, the destruction of the twin towers in New York on 11 September 2001 confirmed warnings of a 'resurgent Islam' and a 'clash of civilizations'.

Muslim leaders have long been concerned about the rise of religious extremism within their community. Radicals express in religious terms socio-political problems that affect their own and other Muslim societies, such as the corruption and repression of Western-supported regimes, some of whose policies are widely regarded as perpetrating injustices upon Muslim peoples in areas such as Palestine, Chechnya, Afghanistan, Algeria, Iraq, and Bosnia. In June 2014 the jihadist so-called 'Islamic State' (IS) group declared the establishment of a 'caliphate' and seized extensive territory in Syria and Iraq.

Sikhism

Sikhism is one of the youngest of the world's major religions. Around 1500 CE, Nanak, the religion's founder, is said to have been transformed by God while bathing. He emerged with the words, 'There is no Hindu, there is no Muslim' – a simple creed that became the basis of Sikhism.

The history of Sikhism has always been closely linked to the Punjab, the land of its origins. Sikhism first emerged in a society that was religiously divided. It is not a mere combination of Hindu and Muslim elements: from the outset it has defined itself as a new and independent third way. Yet it is the product of the relationship, in the Punjab and beyond, of a vigorous minority community with the two larger traditions of Hinduism and Islam.

Guru Nanak (1469–1539) was a capable organizer of his followers as well as an insightful and powerful teacher. He laid the foundations for some of the defining practices of Sikhism, particularly the daily offices of prayer (*nitnem*) and congregational assembly to hear the hymns of the Guru. Guru Nanak went outside his family to select his successor Angad (r. 1539–52) as second Guru of the Sikh community, or *Panth* (path, way).

After Nanak's death, the Sikhs were led by a line of living Gurus until the death of the 10th Guru in 1708. Although the third Guru, Amar Das (r. 1552–74), symbolically rejected the Hindu caste hierarchy by instituting the *langar*, the temple kitchen offering food to all regardless of caste, all the Gurus were from the same Khatri caste as Nanak. From the fifth Guru onwards the succession became hereditary within a single family.

Initially the centre of the community shifted with each Guru, until Guru Arjan (r. 1581–1606) founded the great temple at Amritsar – the Golden Temple (*Harimandir*) – which since its inauguration in 1604 has been the focal point of Sikhism. Guru Arjan also codified the Sikh scriptures, the *Adi Granth* ('original book'). This huge hymnal fills 1,430 pages in the modern edition, and is central to the ritual of Sikh temples (*gurdwara* – 'gate of the Guru').

Guru Gobind Singh and the Khalsa

The *Panth* grew in numbers during the time of the early Gurus, which overlapped with the reign of the great Mughal emperor Akbar (1542–1605). However the strategic location of the Punjab embroiled the Gurus in imperial politics, and Guru Arjan became the first Sikh martyr, when Akbar's less tolerant successor Jehangir executed him for allegedly supporting a rebellion. During the 17th century, continuing conflict with the Mughals resulted in the execution of the 9th Guru, Tegh Bahadur (r. 1664–75), in Delhi.

This led to a radical new formation of the community, under the martyred leader's son, Guru Gobind Singh (r. 1675–1708), the 10th and last Guru. Guru Gobind adopted the role of ruler as well as Guru in his court at Anandpur, in the Punjab. He re-established the Guru's authority over the *Panth* by founding a new order called the *Khalsa*, the Guru's elite. Since the time of the last Guru, baptized members of the *Khalsa* have led the *Panth*. Gobind Singh's sons were killed during his struggles with the Mughal emperor Aurangzeb (1618–1707), and he was himself killed by a Muslim assassin. With his death, the line of living Gurus came to an end; their authority was henceforth vested in the scripture, revered as the Guru Granth Sahib.

During the 18th century, the Punjab was fought over between the declining Mughal Empire and new Muslim invaders from Afghanistan. This was the heroic age of the Sikh *Panth*, who mounted a spirited resistance

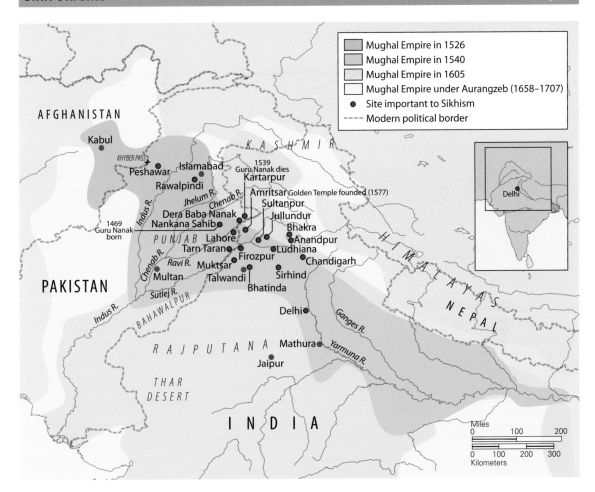

Map legend:
- Mughal Empire in 1526
- Mughal Empire in 1540
- Mughal Empire in 1605
- Mughal Empire under Aurangzeb (1658–1707)
- Site important to Sikhism
- Modern political border

AFGHANISTAN

Kabul

KHYBER PASS

Peshawar
Islamabad
Rawalpindi

KASHMIR

1539
Guru Nanak dies
Kartarpur

Jhelum R.
Chenab R.

Amritsar Golden Temple founded (1577)
Sultanpur
Jullundur

Indus R.

1469
Guru Nanak
born

Dera Baba Nanak
Nankana Sahib

PUNJAB Lahore
Tarn Taran

Chenab R.
Ravi R.

Muktsar

Multan
Talwandi
Bhatinda

Firozpur

Bhakra
Anandpur
Ludhiana
Chandigarh

Sirhind

HIMALAYAS

NEPAL

PAKISTAN

Sutlej R.
BAHAWALPUR

Indus R.

Delhi

RAJPUTANA
Mathura
Jaipur

Ganges R.

Yamuna R.

THAR
DESERT

INDIA

Delhi

Miles
0   100   200

0   100   200   300
Kilometers

to both Muslim armies. Led by the Jat Sikhs, who had become the dominant group in the community, the *Khalsa* forces achieved success with the capture of Lahore, the provincial capital, which became the centre of a powerful Sikh kingdom under Maharaja Ranjit Singh (1799–1839). However his weaker successors were unable to resist the British, who, after two hard-fought wars, incorporated the Punjab into their Indian Empire in 1849.

Modern Sikhism

In the late 19th century, leaders of Indian society, including Sikhs, confronted British political dominance, with its Christian emphasis. After the British conquered Ranjit Singh's kingdom, Sikh religious identity seemed to be threatened by the dismantling of Sikh political institutions, and by a resurgent Hinduism.

Sikh reformist associations (*Singh Sabhas*) formed in the main cities of the Punjab, formulating a redefined Sikhism with a distinctive Sikh identity that has remained the orthodoxy till today. Meanwhile cultural transformation was achieved in the community through reformers such as Bhai Vir Singh (1872–1957).

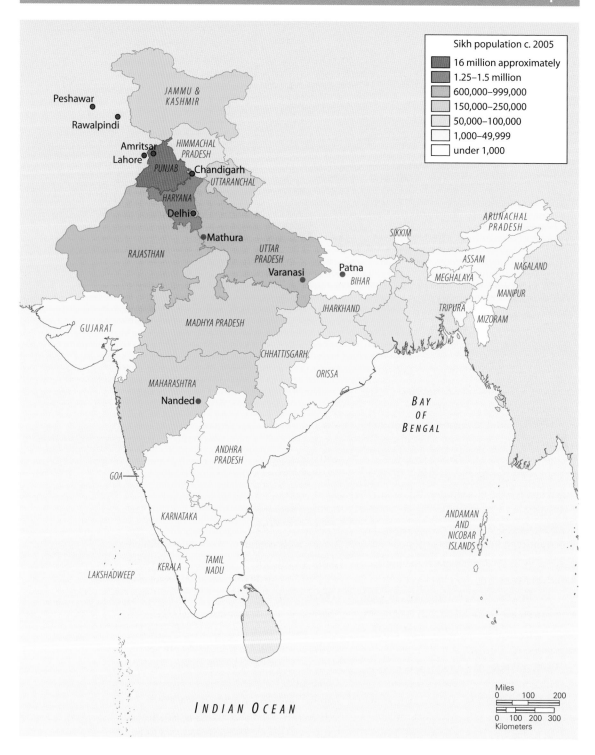

Sikh population c. 2005
- 16 million approximately
- 1.25–1.5 million
- 600,000–999,000
- 150,000–250,000
- 50,000–100,000
- 1,000–49,999
- under 1,000

Peshawar

Rawalpindi

JAMMU & KASHMIR

HIMMACHAL PRADESH

Amritsar
Lahore
PUNJAB
Chandigarh
UTTARANCHAL

HARYANA

Delhi

Mathura

RAJASTHAN

UTTAR PRADESH

Varanasi
Patna
BIHAR

SIKKIM

ARUNACHAL PRADESH

ASSAM

MEGHALAYA

NAGALAND

MANIPUR

TRIPURA

MIZORAM

JHARKHAND

GUJARAT

MADHYA PRADESH

CHHATTISGARH

ORISSA

MAHARASHTRA

Nanded

BAY OF BENGAL

ANDHRA PRADESH

GOA

KARNATAKA

ANDAMAN AND NICOBAR ISLANDS

LAKSHADWEEP

KERALA

TAMIL NADU

INDIAN OCEAN

Miles
0   100   200

0   100   200   300
Kilometers

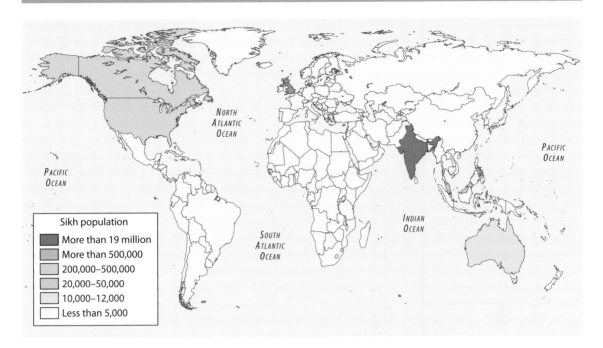

By the end of World War I, reformists had given Sikhs confidence to engage with nationalist politics. The Akali movement transferred control of the major *gurdwaras* from hereditary guardians to an elected committee of male Sikhs, the *Shiromani Gurdwara Prabandhak* Committee (SGPC), which became the most important voice in Sikhism.

With no real chance of achieving their own country, the Sikhs cast their lot with the Hindus in 1947, when partition of the Punjab between India and Pakistan was effected. This uprooted half the community from the Pakistan side to the Indian Punjab, but for the first time consolidated the Sikh population territorially.

From this base, the Akali Dal launched the Punjabi State campaign, aiming to establish a linguistically-defined state with a Sikh majority. By the early 1980s, the Punjab had become a battleground, with Sikh activists fighting Indian security forces, culminating with the Indian prime minister, Indira Gandhi (1917–84) ordering the army to storm the Golden Temple in 1984. Her assassination by Sikh bodyguards provoked anti-Sikh pogroms in many parts of India, and separatism eventually lost the support of most Sikhs in India.

The Sikh diaspora

Increasingly confident and well-established diaspora communities have been settled for more than a generation in Britain, Canada, and the USA, and totals around 1 million. The Sikh diaspora remains closely linked to the Punjab through family ties, the rituals of the *gurdwara*, the great Sikh festivals (*gurpurbs*), and regular pilgrimages to the great shrines. But they are also directly exposed to Western environments and relatively free of the constraints experienced in an increasingly Hindu-dominated India.

Part 7

World Religions Today

Japanese Religions

Religion in Japan is a rich tapestry of diverse traditions. Many people display allegiance to more than one religion: Shinto, Buddhist, and various new religions.

Japan has received much from Korea and China: the main imported religions are Buddhism, mainly in its Mahayana form, and Confucianism. The influence of Taoism has been largely indirect, partly through Zen Buddhism. Japan's native Shinto faith first emerged in reaction to Buddhism and Confucianism, with their scholarly prestige and political influence.

Japan consists of four main islands. The most famous Shinto shrines and Buddhist temples are in the main island, Honshu. Important Shinto shrines are at Ise, where the sun-goddess Amaterasu is revered, and at Izumo, where all the gods, or *kami*, are said to return once a year. The former capitals, Nara and Kyoto, have Shinto shrines, such as the Kasuga Shrine at Nara, and many fine Buddhist temples and images. The island of Shikoku has a famous pilgrim route taking in 88 Buddhist temples. Kyushu, the southernmost island, has some of the oldest sites because of its proximity to Korea. It was the main base for Roman Catholic missions in the 16th century, and for the Shinto-inspired reassertion of imperial power in the mid-19th century.

Japan's mountainous terrain has also influenced the forms of Japanese religious life. Many mountains – most famously Mount Fuji – have shrines that attract pilgrim groups. Mount Koya became one of the centres of Shingon Buddhism.

Shinto

Shinto is the name for a collection of religious practices with roots in prehistoric Japan which were broadly animist, believing a supernatural force resided in natural objects such as mountains, trees, and animals. From the Yamato period onwards, the imperial household was central to Shinto, tracing its roots back to Ninigi, believed to have been grandson of the sun-goddess Amaterasu.

From 1868, when the monarchy was restored to a central position in Japan, until the end of the Pacific War in 1945, the Shinto religion was focused sharply on the emperor cult. After the war, the emperor's semi-divine status was officially denied and Shinto disestablished. Nevertheless, the imperial family still enjoys high esteem, and Shinto shrines remain important symbols of Japanese nationhood.

Today Shinto is based on individual shrines, each of which has a particular reason for its existence, whether it be a natural phenomenon, such as a mountain, a historical event, or an act of personal devotion or political patronage.

Japanese Buddhism

Japanese Buddhism can be traced back to the early 6th century CE, when images and *sutras*, or Buddhist scriptures, were sent from Korea. Prince Shotoku, regent from 593 to 622 CE, established Buddhism as a national religion, linking it to Confucian ideals of morality and statecraft.

A later Buddhist centre drew its inspiration from the Chinese T'ien T'ai school, which became known in Japan as Tendai Buddhism. This in turn was affected by an esoteric form of Buddhism – Shingon – established by the famous monk Kukai (744–835), posthumously known as Kobo Daishi. The Lotus Sutra had already been important in Tendai Buddhism, but Nichiren (1222–82) gave it a new centrality. His writings provided the basis for a number of sects, including influential modern lay Buddhist movements.

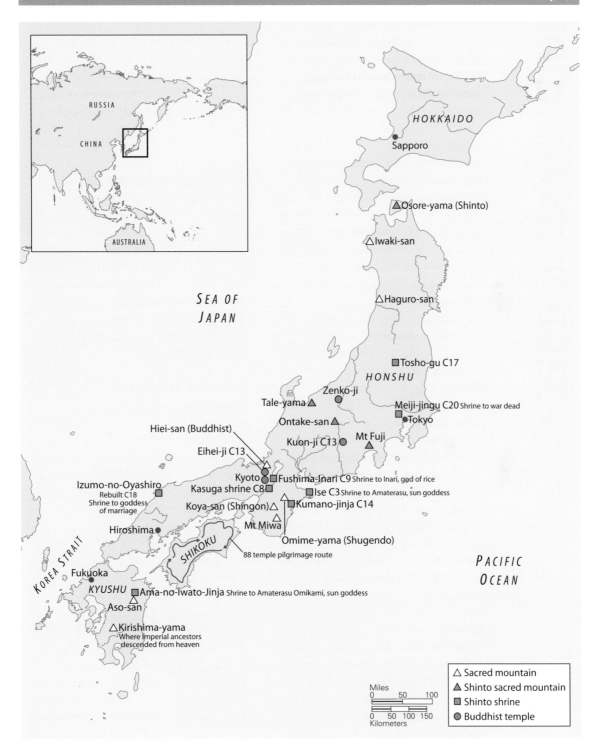

RUSSIA

CHINA

AUSTRALIA

HOKKAIDO

Sapporo

△Osore-yama (Shinto)

△Iwaki-san

SEA OF
JAPAN

△Haguro-san

■Tosho-gu C17

HONSHU

Zenko-ji

Tale-yama △

Meiji-jingu C20 Shrine to war dead

Ontake-san △

■Tokyo

Hiei-san (Buddhist)

Mt Fuji △

Eihei-ji C13

Kuon-ji C13 ●

Kyoto

■Fushima-Inari C9 Shrine to Inari, god of rice

Izumo-no-Oyashiro
Rebuilt C18
Shrine to goddess
of marriage

Kasuga shrine C8 ■

■Ise C3 Shrine to Amaterasu, sun goddess

Koya-san (Shingon)△

■Kumano-jinja C14

Mt Miwa △

Hiroshima ●

SHIKOKU

Omime-yama (Shugendo)

88 temple pilgrimage route

KOREA STRAIT

PACIFIC
OCEAN

Fukuoka ●

KYUSHU ■Ama-no-Iwato-Jinja Shrine to Amaterasu Omikami, sun goddess

△
Aso-san

△Kirishima-yama
Where imperial ancestors
descended from heaven

Miles
0   50   100

0   50   100 150
Kilometers

△ Sacred mountain
▲ Shinto sacred mountain
■ Shinto shrine
● Buddhist temple

Religion in China Today

China has always had its own distinctive religious traditions, in part due to their having developed virtually in isolation from those elsewhere, with none of the idea-sharing common in Western religions. Chinese traditions have tended to focus more on ethics than on speculation about the existence of a deity.

While the ethical teachings of Confucius himself were to some extent amplified by later prophets, especially Mencius and Hsün-tzu, the Taoist religion emerged almost in contrast to Confucianism's emphasis on service to society, concerned with seeking a mystical unity with the Tao – a metaphysical absolute – by the contemplation of nature. Both traditions also changed through the influence of Buddhism. The crossover between these three traditions is such that today many people see no problem in being an adherent of all three. During the 20th century, all three traditions struggled to survive Maoist Communism and the Cultural Revolution, while the re-emergence and rise of Christianity was one result of the relaxation of state proscription.

In the early 20th century, the Chinese regarded Christianity as an imported 'foreign' religion. Today, out of a total population of 1,330 billion in 2010, it has been estimated that approximately 85 million are Protestants, and another 21 million Catholics. If these figures are accurate, China would contain the third largest Christian population in the world, after the USA and Brazil. Chinese Christianity has undergone a process of 'sinicization', or indigenization, becoming embedded in the Chinese culture. The core of state policy towards Christianity in China is the 'Three Self Policy' – self-support, self-government, self-propagation – adopted in the 1950s by all officially-sanctioned religious groups.

MAJOR RELIGIONS OF MODERN CHINA

KAZAKHSTAN

XINJIANG UIGHUR

TIBET

NEPAL

BHUTA

INDIA

BANGLADE

BAY OF BENG

- Roman Catholic
- Protestant
- Buddhist
- Taoist
- Muslim
- No dominant religion/no data

map 51

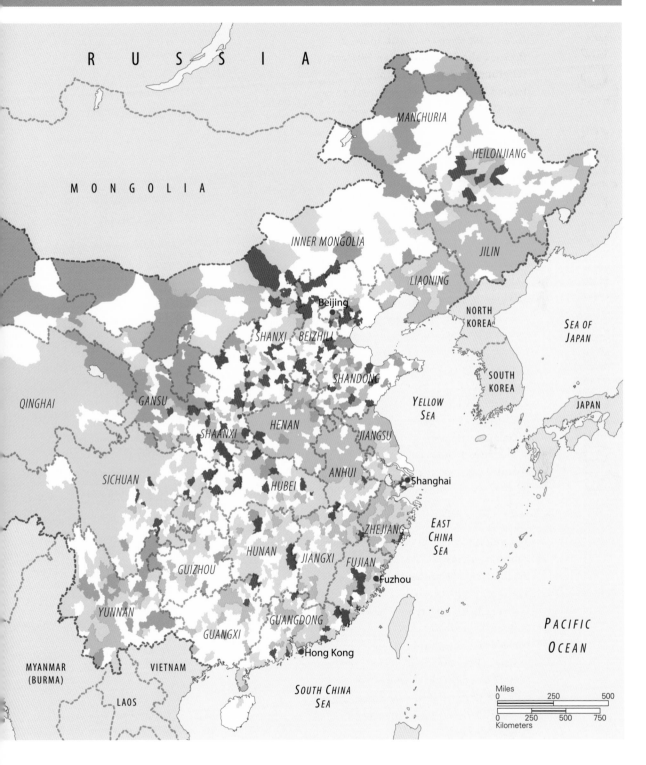

RUSSIA

MONGOLIA

MANCHURIA

HEILONJIANG

INNER MONGOLIA

JILIN

LIAONING

NORTH
KOREA

Beijing

SHANXI BEIZHILI

SHANDONG

SEA OF
JAPAN

SOUTH
KOREA

JAPAN

QINGHAI

GANSU

SHAANXI

HENAN

JIANGSU

YELLOW
SEA

SICHUAN

HUBEI

ANHUI

Shanghai

ZHEJIANG

EAST
CHINA
SEA

HUNAN

JIANGXI

FUJIAN

GUIZHOU

Fuzhou

YUNNAN

GUANGDONG

PACIFIC

OCEAN

GUANGXI

MYANMAR
(BURMA)

VIETNAM

Hong Kong

LAOS

SOUTH CHINA
SEA

Miles
0   250   500

0   250   500   750
Kilometers

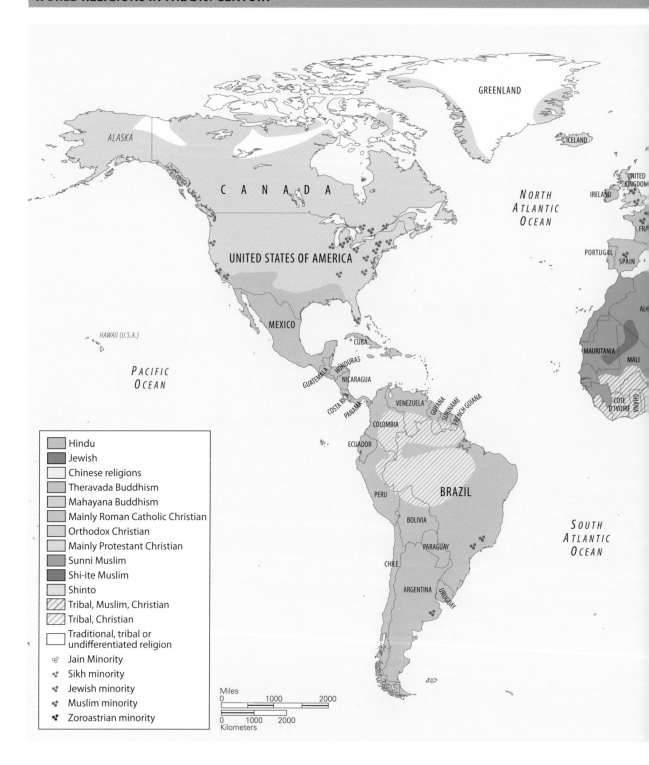

Hindu
Jewish
Chinese religions
Theravada Buddhism
Mahayana Buddhism
Mainly Roman Catholic Christian
Orthodox Christian
Mainly Protestant Christian
Sunni Muslim
Shi-ite Muslim
Shinto
Tribal, Muslim, Christian
Tribal, Christian
Traditional, tribal or undifferentiated religion
Jain Minority
Sikh minority
Jewish minority
Muslim minority
Zoroastrian minority

map 52

SWEDEN
FINLAND

R U S S I A

POLAND
BELARUS
UKRAINE

KHAZAKHSTAN

MONGOLIA

UZBEKISTAN
TURKMENISTAN

TURKEY

SYRIA
IRAQ   IRAN   AFGHANISTAN

CHINA

N. KOREA
S. KOREA   JAPAN

TIBET

PAKISTAN

LIBYA
EGYPT

SAUDI
ARABIA   OMAN

INDIA

BURMA
LAOS

CHAD
SUDAN (N)

YEMEN

ARABIAN
SEA

THAILAND

VIETNAM

PHILIPPINE
IS.

PACIFIC
OCEAN

SUDAN
(S)   ETHIOPIA

SOMALIA

SRI LANKA

D.R.
CONGO

KENYA

INDIAN
OCEAN

MALAYSIA

TANZANIA

INDONESIA

PAPUA
NEW
GUINEA

ANGOLA
ZAMBIA
MOZAMBIQUE
NAMIBIA   ZIMBABWE
BOTSWANA   MADAGASCAR

AUSTRALIA

SOUTH
AFRICA

NEW
ZEALAND

What are Indigenous Religions?

Indigenous religions make up the majority of the world's religions. They are as diverse as the languages spoken, the music made, and the means of subsistence employed by the many people who find them meaningful and satisfying.

Not all indigenous religions are the same. There are hundreds of indigenous languages in, for example, North America and Papua New Guinea; there are also many different ways of being religious.

Few indigenous languages have a word like 'religion', and some scholars have concluded that it is inappropriate to speak of 'religion' when referring to indigenous cultures. But if we think of religions as particular ways of living in and seeing the world, we can find religion in the ordinary, everyday lives of many people who do not use the word.

As a result of the spread of global religions – for example Buddhism, Christianity, and Islam – some indigenous religions have been destroyed, rejected, and abandoned. Some indigenous people have accepted the arriving religion on their own terms, incorporating it into an indigenous understanding. Many indigenous religions have adapted to the presence of more powerful or dominant religions and continued with vitality and creativity. Some people are returning to their 'traditional ways', while others engage in both an indigenous and another newer religion.

Indigenous religions are not the 'fossilized' remains of the earliest, or first, religions. They are rarely simple or simplistic, and should not – as was common among Western scholars in the past – be taken as the basic building blocks from which 'more advanced' religions were built or evolved. Chauvinistic terms such as 'primitive religion' or 'primal religion', commonly used previously, detract from a respectful understanding of the ways in which different people understand and engage with the world. It is also unacceptable to speak of groups that may include millions of people as 'tribes', and of their religions as 'tribal religions'. Indigenous religions are not stuck in the past, nor do they only make sense when practised in their original homelands. Although indigenous religions have been heavily affected by colonialism, they continue to provide resources for people in the new, globalized world.

Some indigenous religions feature teaching about a God who created the world. Others hold that everything we see results from the creative activities of many other persons. Perhaps a single creator, or a creative process, started it all – but life then developed as each living being, or person, played their part. Trees separated sky and land, mountains arose to shape the land, coyote or jaguar or a robin tamed fire, corn taught planting cycles and ceremonies, humans built towns: thus the world became the way it is. Similar processes continue to change the world, making it important that people learn to act responsibly and respectfully. All this is common in a great variety of indigenous religions.

Indigenous religions imply a great variety of creative persons. Some might be recognized as similar to the God whom monotheists acknowledge; others are more polytheistic deities, encountered in the kind of intimate, everyday matters for which some scholars use the word 'immanent' – the divine within the world and everyday experience. Many significant persons are humans: elders, priests, shamans, grandparents, rulers, and so on. Although ancestors are important, among indigenous people this word normally refers to those

from whom a particular person or family is descended, rarely 'all those who have died'.

Some indigenous people believe it is possible to cause harm by performing particular rituals, such as witchcraft and sorcery. Solutions might be found by recourse to diviners or shamans. For the indigenous people, these specialists are adept at finding knowledge unavailable to others, and require

Masai men outside traditional huts, Masai Mara, Kenya.

careful, sometimes frightening, training for their role.

Indigenous religions, like other religions, can be considered to be ways in which particular groups of people seek to improve health, happiness, and even wealth for themselves, their families, and communities.

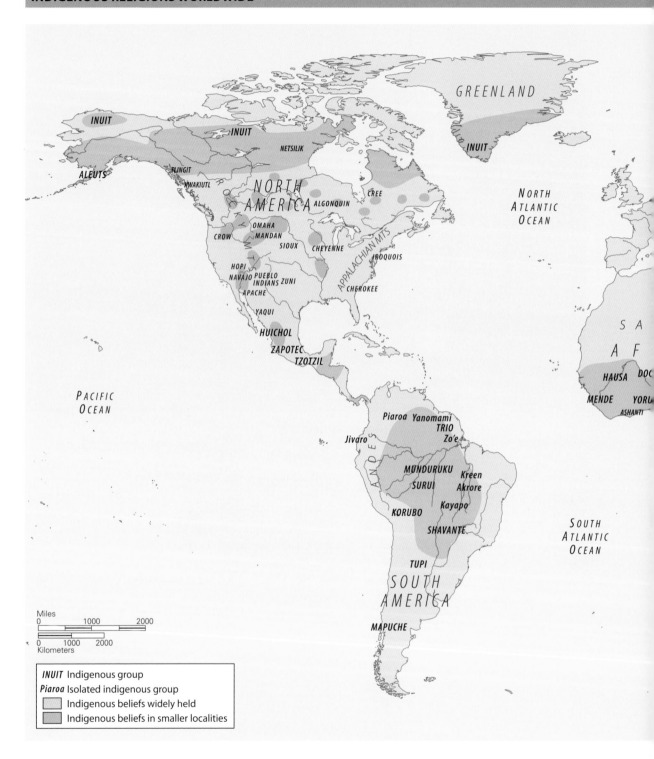

GREENLAND

INUIT

INUIT

INUIT

NETSILIK

ALEUTS

TLINGIT

KWAKIUTL

NORTH
AMERICA

ALGONQUIN

CREE

NORTH
ATLANTIC
OCEAN

OMAHA

CROW

MANDAN

SIOUX

CHEYENNE

APPALACHIAN MTS

IROQUOIS

HOPI

NAVAJO

PUEBLO
INDIANS

ZUNI

APACHE

CHEROKEE

YAQUI

HUICHOL

ZAPOTEC

TZOTZIL

PACIFIC
OCEAN

Piaroa

Yanomami

TRIO

Jivaro

Zo'e

ANDES

MUNDURUKU

Kreen
Akrore

SURUI

KORUBO

Kayapo

SHAVANTE

SOUTH
ATLANTIC
OCEAN

TUPI

SOUTH
AMERICA

MAPUCHE

S A

A F

HAUSA

DOG

MENDE

YORU

ASHANTI

Miles
0   1000   2000

0   1000   2000
Kilometers

INUIT Indigenous group
Piaroa Isolated indigenous group
Indigenous beliefs widely held
Indigenous beliefs in smaller localities

map 53

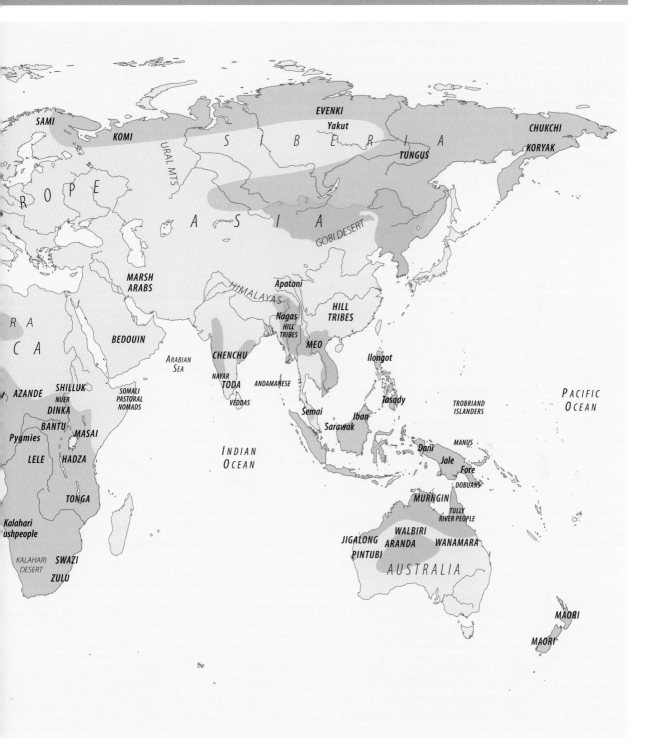

SAMI
KOMI
URAL MTS.
ROPE
RA
CA
AZANDE
SHILLUK
NUER
DINKA
BANTU
Pygmies
MASAI
LELE
HADZA
TONGA
Kalahari
Bushpeople
KALAHARI
DESERT
SWAZI
ZULU

EVENKI
Yakut
SIBERIA
TUNGUS
CHUKCHI
KORYAK

ASIA
GOBI DESERT

MARSH
ARABS
HIMALAYAS
Apatani
Nagas
HILL
TRIBES
HILL
TRIBES
MEO
BEDOUIN
ARABIAN
SEA
CHENCHU
NAYAR
TODA
ANDAMANESE
VEDDAS
SOMALI
PASTORAL
NOMADS

Ilongot
Semai
Tasady
Iban
Sarawak
TROBRIAND
ISLANDERS
PACIFIC
OCEAN

INDIAN
OCEAN
Dani
Jale
MANUS
Fore
DOBUANS
MURNGIN
TULLY
RIVER PEOPLE
WALBIRI
JIGALONG
ARANDA
WANAMARA
PINTUBI
AUSTRALIA

MAORI
MAORI

The term 'New Religious Movements' (NRMs) covers a variety of religious organizations that have emerged and which are often dismissively referred to by mainline religions, particularly the Roman Catholic Church, as 'cults'. Some scholars define a new religion as an organization that has arrived in the West since World War II, while others regard 'new' as covering the last 150 years.

NRMs are a global phenomenon: it is estimated that there are some 10,000 NRMs in Africa, around 3,000 in the USA, and 500–600 in Britain. NRMs tend to fall outside mainstream religion, sometimes because of doctrinal disputes or controversial practices.

19th century NRMs in the West were predominantly Christian. William Miller (1782–1849) proclaimed that Christ's second coming was imminent. He named 1843, subsequently 1844, as the year of Christ's return; his followers' disillusionment in 1844 became known as the 'Great Disappointment'. Ellen G. White (1827–1915), who founded the Seventh-day Adventists in 1861, taught that Jesus had returned, but his presence was invisible.

Charles Taze Russell (1852–1916), who co-founded Zion's Watch Tower Tract Society in 1881, also taught Christ's 'invisible presence', although the Jehovah's Witnesses, as Russell's successor Joseph Rutherford (1869–1942) renamed them in 1931, now date this event to 1914.

Another significant movement was New Thought, or Higher Thought, which taught that Infinite Intelligence – or God – is everywhere, and emphasized health improvement through mental 'affirmations'. These ideas influenced Mary Baker Eddy's (1821–1910) Christian Science movement and the Hopkins Metaphysical Association, set up by Emma Curtis Hopkins (1849–1925)

NEW RELIGIOUS MOVEMENTS WORLDWIDE

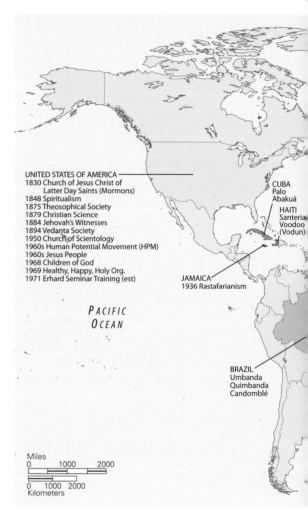

UNITED STATES OF AMERICA
1830 Church of Jesus Christ of
     Latter Day Saints (Mormons)
1848 Spiritualism
1875 Theosophical Society
1879 Christian Science
1884 Jehovah's Witnesses
1894 Vedanta Society
1950 Church of Scientology
1960s Human Potential Movement (HPM)
1960s Jesus People
1968 Children of God
1969 Healthy, Happy, Holy Org.
1971 Erhard Seminar Training (est)

CUBA
Palo
Abakuá

HAITI
Santeria
Voodoo
(Vodun)

JAMAICA
1936 Rastafarianism

BRAZIL
Umbanda
Quimbanda
Candomblé

PACIFIC
OCEAN

Miles
0   1000   2000

0   1000 2000
Kilometers

in 1887. Some of Hopkins' students set up their own organizations, best known of which is the Unity School of Christianity, or Unity Church, founded in Kansas City, Missouri, in 1889.

Modern spiritualism can be traced back to 'rappings' heard by the Fox sisters of Hydesville, New York, in 1848, though modern spiritualist churches emphasize healing as much as contact with the departed. Helena P. Blavatsky (1831–91), one of the founders of the Theosophical

map 54

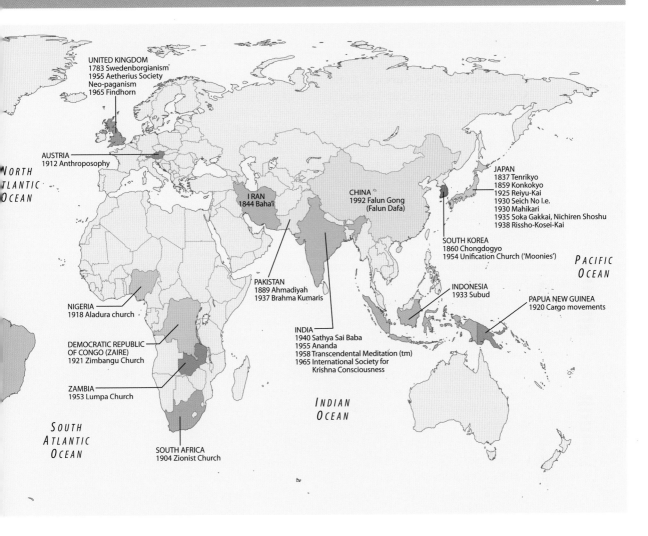

UNITED KINGDOM
1783 Swedenborgianism
1955 Aetherius Society
Neo-paganism
1965 Findhorn

AUSTRIA
1912 Anthroposophy

NORTH
ATLANTIC
OCEAN

IRAN
1844 Baha'i

CHINA
1992 Falun Gong
(Falun Dafa)

JAPAN
1837 Tenrikyo
1859 Konkokyo
1925 Reiyu-Kai
1930 Seich No I.e.
1930 Mahikari
1935 Soka Gakkai, Nichiren Shoshu
1938 Rissho-Kosei-Kai

SOUTH KOREA
1860 Chongdogyo
1954 Unification Church ('Moonies')

PACIFIC
OCEAN

PAKISTAN
1889 Ahmadiyah
1937 Brahma Kumaris

INDONESIA
1933 Subud

PAPUA NEW GUINEA
1920 Cargo movements

NIGERIA
1918 Aladura church

DEMOCRATIC REPUBLIC
OF CONGO (ZAIRE)
1921 Zimbangu Church

INDIA
1940 Sathya Sai Baba
1955 Ananda
1958 Transcendental Meditation (tm)
1965 International Society for
Krishna Consciousness

ZAMBIA
1953 Lumpa Church

INDIAN
OCEAN

SOUTH
ATLANTIC
OCEAN

SOUTH AFRICA
1904 Zionist Church

Society, claimed contact with a number of 'Ascended Masters' – advanced spiritual beings who once lived on earth. Ascended Masters – sometimes called the 'Great White Brotherhood' – also feature in the Rosicrucians, the Church Universal and Triumphant, and the New Age 'channelling' movement.

NRMs in the 1960s and 1970s

A new wave of NRMs occurred in the 1960s. Bible-based and charismatic, the 'Jesus Movement', or 'Jesus People', gained momentum within the youth counter-culture, sometimes involving communal living and sharing of possessions. Converts had often previously been on drugs, and the Love Family, or Church of Jesus Christ at Armageddon, founded in 1968 by Paul Erdman (1940–2007), encouraged their use.

Of the communal groups, the best known are The Family International (TFI), previously known as the Children of God, or COG, and The Holy Spirit Association for the Unification of World Christianity, or Unification Church (UC). Founded by David Brandt Berg ('Moses David', 1919–94), COG was ostensibly Protestant fundamentalist, but became controversial for its 'flirty fishing' – or 'FFing' – offering sex to seekers, mainly by female members. The founder-leader of the Unification Church, Sun Myung Moon (1920–2012), claimed Jesus was unable to accomplish his messianic mission, which was to marry and beget sinless children. He and his wife are regarded as the new messiahs.

Indian-derived NRMs

The first Hindu *swami* (world-renouncer) to visit the West was Ramakrishna's pupil Swami Vivekananda (1863–1902), who founded the Vedanta Society in New York in 1894. Other gurus followed, notably Paramahansa Yogananda (1893–1952), founder of the Self-Realization Fellowship in 1920; Meher Baba (1894–1969), who in 1954 declared he was the Avatar of the age; the Maharishi Mahesh Yogi (1918–2008), who developed the Transcendental Meditation (Transcendental Meditation®) technique; Sri Chinmoy (1931–2007), who promoted 'inner peace'; Swami A. C. Bhaktivedanta Praphupada (1896–1977), founder of the International Society for Krishna Consciousness (ISKCON), better known as the 'Hare Krishna' movement; and Prem Pal Singh Rawat (b. 1957, formerly known as Guru Maharaj Ji), leader of the Elan Vital movement and its predecessor, the Divine Light Mission (DLM). Sathya Sai Baba (1926–2011) never visited the West, but was well known as a miracle-worker. He claimed to be the reincarnation of Sai Baba of Shirdi (d. 1918), an avatar, spiritual saint, and miracle worker.

Bhagavan Shri Rajneesh (1931–90), later known as Osho, taught an idiosyncratic form of Zen Buddhism and celebrated sexual freedom and materialism. In 1981 Rajneesh moved to Oregon, USA, where he set up his 'enlightened city', Rajneeshpuram. Following conflict with locals, Osho was arrested in 1985, and the community disbanded.

Buddhist NRMs

Arriving in the USA in 1897, D. T. Suzuki (1870–1966) wrote prolifically on Zen. The 1960s US youth counter-culture took the Zen notion of the 'Buddha within' to mean promiscuity, and their counter-cultural version of Zen is sometimes known as 'Beat Zen'.

Buddhist NRMs derive from various traditions. The Vipassana movement promotes a Theravada meditative practice. Innovative forms of Tibetan Buddhism include the New Kadampa Tradition (NKT), founded by Geshe Kelsang Gyatso (b. 1931), which became controversial because of a practice known as Dorje Shugden, opposed by the Dalai Lama.

The Soka Gakkai International (SGI), founded in 1930, derives its teachings from the Japanese teacher Nichiren (1222–82) and the Lotus Sutra. The Friends of the Western Buddhist Order (FWBO) seek to develop a new form of Buddhism for Westerners. Founded by the Venerable Sangharakshita (Dennis Lingwood, b. 1925), it emphasizes 'right livelihood' instead of the monastic practice of seeking alms from lay supporters.

Falun Gong, founded in 1992 in China by Li Hongzhi (b. 1951), offers a set of physical exercises similar to tai ch'i, with a path to becoming a Buddha.

The Bahá'í

Sayyid 'Ali Muhammad, born in Shiraz, Persia (modern Iran) in 1819, claimed to be a Messenger of God, and called himself the Báb, meaning 'the gate', but was executed in 1850. Mirza Husayn 'Ali Nuri (1817–92) became a follower of the Báb, took the name

Bahá'u'lláh, and founded the Bahá'í faith. He claimed to be the bearer of a new message from God, built on the previous religions of the world and destined to take humanity to its next stage of development: world unity. His shrine, near Akko, Israel, is the holiest site for Bahá'ís, and the world centre of the Bahá'í faith is in the same area. By the early 21st century more than 5 million Bahá'ís were living in more than 230 countries, with the largest community in India.

Other NRMs

Starting in Jamaica, the Rastafarians were initially a Black Power movement supported by the descendants of slaves. They interpreted the Bible's teachings as pointing to Ethiopia, where they believed Emperor Haile Selassie (1891–1975) was their messiah who would herald a return to Africa. Following his death, a variety of expectations arose.

'UFO religions' hold that the gods are extra-terrestrials who communicate with key humans. The earliest UFO religion in the West was the Aetherius Society, established by George King (1919–97) in 1955. The Raëlian Movement, founded in 1974 by Claude Vorihon (b. 1946) promotes human cloning as the key to personal immortality.

The science fiction writer L. Ron Hubbard (1911–86) came to prominence in 1950 with his best-selling self-improvement book *Dianetics*, the sourcebook of the Church of Scientology. Scientology is one of several groups forming the Human Potential Movement (HPM), organizations that claim to offer enhanced quality of life, such as Erhard Seminar Training (est – now Landmark Forum) founded by Werner Erhard (b. 1935), and the School of Economic Science (SES), which is influenced by Advaita Vedanta.

The Human Potential Movement merges into the nebulous New Age Movement (NAM), which is characterized by eclecticism, optimism about human nature, and disenchantment with organized religion. 'New Age' flourished after 1970, evolving into a more mainstream series of spiritual self-improvement disciplines and quests. Its roots include pagan, Jewish, and Christian Hermetic movements and the occult.

Modern Pilgrimage

Pilgrimage is normally a journey to a holy place, undertaken as a commemoration of a past event, as a celebration, or as an act of penance. The goal can be a natural feature such as a sacred river or mountain, the location of a miracle, revelation, or theophany, or the tomb of a hero or saint.

Hinduism has always promoted pilgrimage to sacred sites. In recent times there has been a growing interest in pilgrimage to shrines such as the Sabarimala Temple in Kerala, and great festivals such as the Kumbh Mela. There has also been an increase in pilgrims visiting gurus in search of miracles.

Similarly Buddhists today go on pilgrimage to holy sites such as Mount Shatrunjaya, in Gujarat, or Shravana Belagola, in Karnataka.

Although the Japanese island of Shikoku lacks major religious monuments, it boasts a famous pilgrimage route which takes in 88 Buddhist temples that are frequently visited by tourists. There are other pilgrimage routes elsewhere in Japan, the most famous being 33 places in western Honshu where the Bodhisattva Kannon-sama is revered.

Pilgrimage has for centuries been important in Christianity, nourished by the belief that a visit to a great shrine could bring physical and spiritual healing. In the Middle Ages pilgrimage to the Holy Land was hard and dangerous, restricted to the very devout and those obliged to do penance for serious sins. Alternative popular shrines included Rome, Canterbury – site of the murder of Thomas Becket in 1170 – and Santiago de Compostela, north-west Spain, by tradition the burial place of St James. Pilgrims tended to travel in groups, gossiping, singing, and stopping at minor shrines along the way.

Modern pilgrimage

Many traditional pilgrimage destinations are still active today, and the ease of long-distance travel can enable mass movements of people. The annual Muslim *hajj* to Mecca now numbers nearly 3 million pilgrims, and the Vatican City, Rome, and the healing shrine at Lourdes in France attract similar numbers.

There are also many new pilgrimages. A modern phenomenon is the link between pilgrimage in the traditional religious sense and sightseeing tourism to religious sites, to appreciate their art, architecture, and culture.

One popular modern Catholic pilgrimage site is the Marian shrine at Knock, Eire, which started with an apparition of the Virgin Mary, St Joseph, and St John in 1879. Knock has attracted increasing numbers of pilgrims,

Pilgrims on the Camino de Santiago, Spain.

particularly since Pope John Paul II visited in 1979 for its centenary.

A controversial site at Medjugorje, Herzegovina, attracts many Catholic pilgrims, after six children claimed to have seen a vision of the Virgin Mary there in 1981 – though the Roman Catholic Church has never officially recognized their claims.

A modern Anglican Christian pilgrimage centre, also revered by Roman Catholics, is the restored medieval shrine of Our Lady of Walsingham, Norfolk, England. The shrine, established in 1061, fell into neglect after the Reformation, but was revived in 1897 by a procession of pilgrims from nearby King's Lynn. Today, thousands of pilgrims, mostly from English parishes, journey to Walsingham each year.

The Taizé community in Burgundy, France, has become one of the world's most important sites of Christian pilgrimage. More than 100,000 young people from around the world make pilgrimages there every year to pray, sing, study the Bible, and do communal work. Through the community's ecumenical outlook, they are encouraged to live in a spirit of kindness, simplicity, and reconciliation.

Muslim Pilgrimages

Although the Muslim *hajj* (pilgrimage) to Mecca is required once in every Muslim's life, Muslims also visit shrines and cemeteries where *walis* (saints) repose. Such a visit is known in Arabic as *ziyara*. Shi'ite and Sunni Muslims make *ziyaras* to Medina, where the Prophet and many other early Muslim saints are buried. Shi'ites also visit Karbala', in Iraq, where Husayn, the Prophet Muhammad's grandson, was martyred; Najaf, where the fourth Imam Ali is buried; and shrines in Iran. Sunni Muslims also make *ziyaras* to shrines throughout the Islamic world.

Indonesians honour nine saints – known as *Wali Songa* – who, according to tradition, brought Islam to Java in the 15th century. Egyptian Muslims venerate many saints in village tombs as well as in major cities. The shrine-tomb of Sidi Ahmed al-Badawi, in the Nile delta city of Tanta, attracts millions of Egyptian pilgrims to the saint's annual birthday celebration.

In South, South-east, and East Asia, huge numbers of Hindus, Buddhists, Shintoists, Confucians, Taoists, and other religious followers continue to participate in pilgrimages. Among the most impressive are the Hindu gathering of Kumbh Mela, which attracts around 70 million at its major festival every 12 years, and the annual Chinese Spring Festival, when around 32 million people travel across the country each year to celebrate the New Year in their family homes.

New Pilgrimages

Towards the end of summer thousands of people from around the world travel to the Black Rock Desert in Nevada, USA, to take part in the Burning Man Festival. This event has no specific religious meaning; it started in 1986 on a San Francisco beach, when a human effigy was burned on the summer solstice accompanied by spontaneous music-making, dancing, and community feeling. In 1990 the event moved to Black Rock, where it is now held annually. One of the attractions is the demanding travel required to reach the festival site, located in the hot desert. Burning Man is a new kind of secular, pilgrimage-passage rite, combining spirituality, tourism, risk, separation, artistic expression, entertainment, and renewal. In Europe, many annual music festivals, notably Glastonbury, display similar characteristics.

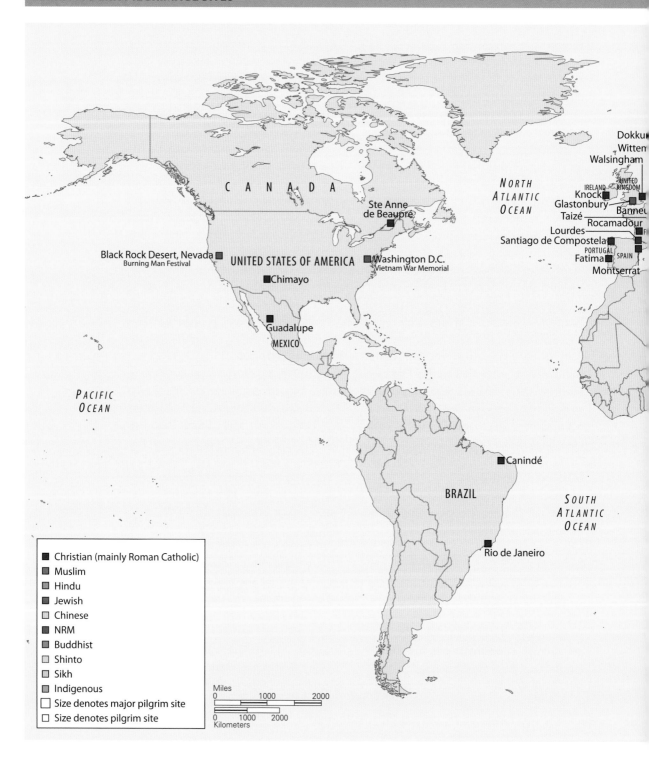

Dokku
Witten
Walsingham

NORTH
ATLANTIC
OCEAN

IRELAND   UNITED
Knock   KINGDOM
Glastonbury   Bannel
Taizé
Rocamadour
Lourdes
Santiago de Compostela
PORTUGAL   SPAIN
Fatima
Montserrat

Ste Anne
de Beaupré

CANADA

Black Rock Desert, Nevada
Burning Man Festival

UNITED STATES OF AMERICA   Washington D.C.
Vietnam War Memorial

Chimayo

Guadalupe

MEXICO

PACIFIC
OCEAN

Canindé

BRAZIL

SOUTH
ATLANTIC
OCEAN

Rio de Janeiro

■ Christian (mainly Roman Catholic)
■ Muslim
■ Hindu
■ Jewish
□ Chinese
■ NRM
■ Buddhist
□ Shinto
□ Sikh
■ Indigenous
□ Size denotes major pilgrim site
□ Size denotes pilgrim site

Miles
0   1000   2000

0   1000   2000
Kilometers

map 55

R U S S I A

CHINA

JAPAN

oreto
Medjugorje
ITALY
me
Mt Athos
GREECE
Jerusalem
Bethlehem
Hebron
Karbala'
Mt Sinai/
ebel Musa
Tanta
Najaf
EGYPT
Luxor
SAUDI ARABIA
Ziyarat
Medina
Mecca

Mashhad
IRAN
Qom

Kedarnath
Gangotri
Yamnotri
Amritsar
Rishikesh
Haridwar
Badrinath
Sarnath
INDIA
Varanasi
(Benares)
Sabarimala
Tirupati

ARABIAN
SEA

Mt Kailas
Mt Nanda Devi
Lhasa
Mt Kangchenjunga
Kathmandu
Bodh Gaya

Chinese Spring Festival
C H I N A
Tai Shan
Wen Shu

Mt Fuji
Shikoku

Kandy
SRI LANKA
Sri Pada

INDIAN
OCEAN

PACIFIC
OCEAN

AUSTRALIA
Ayers Rock

Jerusalem: The Holy City

Jerusalem is the city of kings David and Solomon, the See of Greek Orthodox, Armenian, and Roman Catholic patriarchs and of an Anglican bishop, and a holy city for Muslims. It boasts innumerable holy places sacred to the three great monotheistic religions.

The Old City of Jerusalem is an area of only 220 acres (one square kilometre), bounded by walls constructed by the Ottoman Turks in the 16th century, but contains numerous sacred sites — Christian, Jewish, and Islamic.

Dominating the Old City is the vast *Haram Al Sharif*, or Noble Sanctuary, the site of the Islamic Dome of the Rock and the *Al-Aqsa* Mosque, but in biblical times the location of the Jewish Temple. Within the Old City are remains of fortifications dating from Old Testament times, Hasmonean relics, Herodian ruins, Roman arches and columns, Byzantine churches, sites revered for centuries by Christians as associated with Jesus, early Christian sanctuaries, Arab shrines, Crusader relics, and Mameluk fortifications.

Jerusalem is situated on twin ridges roughly 2,700 feet (830 metres) above sea level, divided by the Tyropoeon Valley. To its east the Old City is bounded by the Kidron Valley, and to the west and south by the Hinnom Valley. On Mount Ophel, where the three valleys join, King David captured the Jebusite city, making it his capital city. The Temple area, first enclosed by David's son Solomon, is visible today as the Temple Mount, or *Haram al-Sharif*, the great platform on which the Dome of the Rock stands. Solomon's Temple was destroyed when Nebuchadnezzar took Jerusalem in 586 BCE. After the Babylonian exile, many people of Judah returned to the city in 538 BCE to rebuild the temple, and, under Nehemiah's leadership, to strengthen the city's defences. Some evidence of this period can still be seen.

One of Herod the Great's public works was to rebuild the temple more grandiosely. After the Roman general Vespasian subdued the Jewish Revolt of 66 CE, his son Titus took Jerusalem and burned down the temple. Following the defeat of the Bar Kokhba revolt (132–35 CE), the Emperor Hadrian razed Jerusalem to the ground and laid out a new city, Aelia Capitolina, from which all Jews were banished. The grid-pattern of his city is reflected in the layout of the present Old City.

After Emperor Constantine declared Christianity a legal religion, Jerusalem began to become the centre of the Christian world. Churches were constructed over the major sites of Christian significance, such as Golgotha, the Holy Sepulchre, Gethsemane, and the Mount of Olives.

In 638 Jerusalem was captured by the Muslim Arabs. Although the new ruler, Caliph Omar, did not to stop Christians praying in the Church of the Holy Sepulchre, he set up a small mosque on the site of the present Al-Aqsa. In 691 CE Caliph Abd al-Malik ibn Marwan completed the Dome of the Rock on the Temple Mount, and it has dominated the Jerusalem skyline ever since.

In 1009 the Crusaders captured the city from the Arabs. They built several new churches, notably the Church of St Anne. After a long struggle, the Crusaders were expelled again in 1187, and the city was controlled by the Ayyubids and Mamluks.

In 1517 the Ottoman Sultan Selim captured the city. His son, Suleiman I, 'the Magnificent' (r. 1520–66), rebuilt the gates and walls, leaving them much as they appear today.

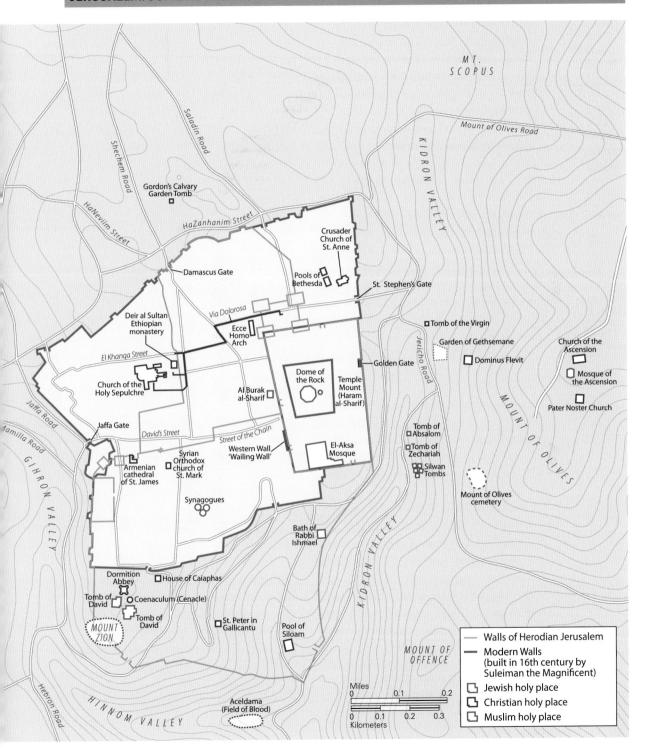

MT.
SCOPUS

Mount of Olives Road

KIDRON VALLEY

Saladin Road

Shechem Road

HaNeviim Street

Gordon's Calvary
Garden Tomb

HaZanhanim Street

Damascus Gate

Crusader
Church of
St. Anne

Pools of
Bethesda

St. Stephen's Gate

Via Dolorosa

Deir al Sultan
Ethiopian
monastery

Ecce
Homo
Arch

Tomb of the Virgin

Jericho Road

Garden of Gethsemane

Church of the
Ascension

El Khanqa Street

Golden Gate

Dominus Flevit

Mosque of
the Ascension

Church of the
Holy Sepulchre

Al Burak
al-Sharif

Dome of
the Rock

Temple
Mount
(Haram
al-Sharif)

Pater Noster Church

MOUNT OF OLIVES

Jaffa Road

Jaffa Gate

David's Street

Street of the Chain

Western Wall
'Wailing Wall'

El-Aksa
Mosque

Tomb of
Absalom

Tomb of
Zechariah

Mamilla Road

Syrian
Orthodox
church of
St. Mark

Armenian
cathedral
of St. James

Silwan
Tombs

GIHON VALLEY

Synagogues

Mount of Olives
cemetery

Bath of
Rabbi
Ishmael

KIDRON VALLEY

Dormition
Abbey

House of Caiaphas

Tomb of
David

Coenaculum (Cenacle)

Tomb of
David

St. Peter in
Gallicantu

Pool of
Siloam

MOUNT
ZION

MOUNT OF
OFFENCE

Hebron Road

HINNOM VALLEY

Aceldama
(Field of Blood)

Miles
0   0.1   0.2

0   0.1   0.2   0.3
Kilometers

Walls of Herodian Jerusalem

Modern Walls
(built in 16th century by
Suleiman the Magnificent)

Jewish holy place

Christian holy place

Muslim holy place

What is the *Hajj*?

One of the five fundamental duties of Islamic worship – to be fulfilled once in a lifetime if possible – is the *Hajj*, the pilgrimage to Mecca and its vicinity, home of the holiest sites for Muslims. Mecca has associations with Muhammad, who began his life in the city, and also with his precursor, Abraham, who, according to the *Qur'an*, built the *Ka'ba*, helped by his son, Ishmael.

A visit to Mecca has religious significance for Muslims at any time of year. But in the 12th month of the Muslim calendar the season of the *Hajj*, or Great Pilgrimage, arrives. Pilgrims come to Mecca in their millions, wearing simple pilgrimage clothing of white cloth. They congregate in the Great Mosque and perform the first rite of pilgrimage – the *tawaf*, during which pilgrims circumambulate the *Ka'ba* anti-clockwise seven times. They next run seven times between two small hills, recalling the plight of Hagar and her son, Ishmael, who, in Islamic, Jewish, and Christian tradition, were saved from death by a spring of water that God revealed in the desert sands. This well is named in the Islamic tradition as *zamzam*.

Next pilgrims walk a few miles outside Mecca to Mount Arafat, where the *Hajj* comes to its climax. Here pilgrims 'stand' in meditation before God from midday to sunset. Then they begin the return journey to Mecca, stopping overnight at Muizdalifah, where each pilgrim gathers pebbles. The next day, they throw these pebbles ritually against three stone pillars in the neighbouring village of Mina, recalling when Abraham resisted Satan's temptations to disobey after God instructed him to prepare his son Ishmael for sacrifice, as a test of his obedience (*islam*).

THE ROUTE OF THE *HAJJ*

Al Haram

Ka'ba

MECCA

① Day one. Put on the *ihram*, and go from Mecca to Mina before noon

⑥ Cut or shave hair, remove *ihram*, offer animal sacrifice and go to Mecca to perform *tawaf-i-infadah*, circling Ka'ba 7 times

Miles
0   1   2

0   1   2   3
Kilometers

The *Qur'an* says the boy was ransomed 'with a tremendous victim'. In recollection of this, pilgrims offer the sacrifice of sheep or camels. The final day, *Eid al-Adha*, the Festival of the Sacrifice, commemorates Abraham's willingness to sacrifice his son.

map 57

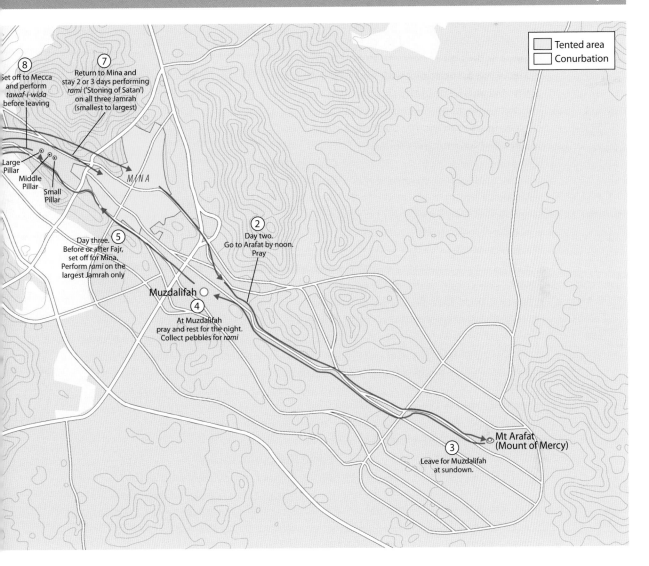

Tented area
Conurbation

⑧ Set off to Mecca and perform *tawaf-i-wida* before leaving

⑦ Return to Mina and stay 2 or 3 days performing *rami* ('Stoning of Satan') on all three Jamrah (smallest to largest)

Large Pillar
Middle Pillar
Small Pillar

MINA

② Day two. Go to Arafat by noon. Pray

⑤ Day three. Before or after Fajr, set off for Mina. Perform *rami* on the largest Jamrah only

Muzdalifah ○

④ At Muzdalifah pray and rest for the night. Collect pebbles for *rami*

Mt Arafat (Mount of Mercy)

③ Leave for Muzdalifah at sundown.

Further Reading

Religious Studies

Chryssides, George D., *The Study of Religion*, 2nd revised ed. London: Bloomsbury Academic, 2013.

Connolly, Peter (ed.), *Approaches to the Study of Religion*. London: Continuum, 2001.

Fitzgerald, Timothy, *The Ideology of Religious Studies*. Oxford: Oxford University Press, 2000.

Pals, Daniel L. *Eight Theories of Religion*. New York: Oxford University Press, 2006.

Partridge, Christopher ed., rev. Tim Dowley, *Introduction to World Religions,* 4th ed. Minneapolis: Fortress Press, 2014.

The Ancient World

Beard, Mary, J. North, and S. Price, *Religions of Rome*, 2 vols. Cambridge: Cambridge University Press, 1998.

Easterling, P. E. and J. V. Muir, *Greek Religion and Society*. Cambridge: Cambridge University Press, 1985.

Hart, George: *Egyptian Myths*. Austin: University of Texas Press, 1997.

Rose, Jenny, *Zoroastrianism: An Introduction*. London: I. B. Tauris, 2011.

Hinduism

Lopez, Donald S. Jr., ed., *Religions of India in Practice*. Princeton: Princeton University Press, 1995.

Mittal, S., G. Thursby, eds., *The Hindu World*. New York: Routledge, 2004.

Buddhism

Lopez, Donald S. Jr., *The Story of Buddhism: A Concise Guide to its History and Teachings*. New York: HarperCollins, 2002.

Williams, Paul, *Buddhist Thought: A Complete Introduction to the Indian Tradition*. New York: Routledge, 2000.

Judaism

Biale, David, ed., *Cultures of the Jews: A New History*. New York: Schocken Books, 2002.

Schama, Simon, *The Story of the Jews and the Fate of the World*. London: Bodley Head, 2013.

Christianity

Dowley, Tim, ed., *Introduction to the History of Christianity*. 2nd ed. Minneapolis: Fortress Press, 2014.

Hastings, Adrian, ed., *A World History of Christianity*. Grand Rapids, Michigan: Wm. B. Eerdmans, 1999.

MacCulloch, Diarmaid: *A History of Christianity: The First Three Thousand Years*. London: Penguin, 2009.

Islam

Aslan, Reza, *No God but God: The Origins, Evolution, and Future of Islam*. New York: Random House, 2006.

Esposito, John, ed., *The Oxford Encyclopedia of the Modern Islamic World*. New York: Oxford University Press, 1995.

World Religions Today

Bowker, John, ed., *Oxford Dictionary of World Religions*. Oxford: Oxford University Press, 1997.

Chryssides, George D., *A Reader in New Religious Movements*. London: Continuum, 2006.

Gazetteer

Note: numbers are map numbers, not page numbers

Abidjan
worldwide Christian missions in the early 20th century 36

Abu (mount)
Jainism in India 12

Abu Simbel
Ancient Egypt 3

Abydos
Ancient Egypt 3

Abyssinia
journeys of Muhammad 39

Acco
Exodus 18
Kingdoms of Saul, David, and Solomon 19

Aceh
spread of Islam in South-east Asia 42

Acerenza
church in 1050 33

Achaia
Jews and Christians in the 1st century 29
spread of Christianity by 325 CE 30

Addis Ababa
worldwide Christian missions in the early 20th century 36

Aden
journeys of Muhammad 39

Adiabene
spread of Christianity by 325 CE 30

Adrianopolis
spread of Christianity by 325 CE 30

Aegean Sea
Jews and Christians in the 1st century 29

Aegina
Jews and Christians in the 1st century 29

Aegyptus
Jews and Christians in the 1st century 29
spread of Christianity by 325 CE 30

Aenon
Palestine in the time of Christ 28

Afghanistan
Muslim peoples of modern Asia 45

Africa
spread of Islam 44

Agade
Mesopotamia 2

Ahichchhatra
Buddhist heartland 13

Ahmadabad
Islamic expansion in India 41

Ahwas
Jews and Islam 22

Aihole
Temple Hinduism 9
world religions 600 BCE–600 CE 32

Aila
journeys of Muhammad 39

Ajmer
Islamic expansion in India 41
world religions 1500 43

Al Qudisiya
spread of Islam by 750 CE 40

Al Raji
journeys of Muhammad 39

Al-'Ula
journeys of Muhammad 39

Alampur
Temple Hinduism 9

Alba Iulia
world religions 600 BCE–600 CE 32

Albany
origins of Judaism in the USA 25

Alderney
Judaism and the Third Reich 26

Aleppo
Jewish exiles 20
Jews and Islam 22
Kingdoms of Saul, David, and Solomon 19
spread of Islam by 750 CE 40

Alexandria
Christianity in the 4th and 5th centuries 31
Jewish diaspora 21
Jewish exiles 20
Jews and Christians in the 1st century 29
Roman religion 6
spread of Christianity by 325 CE 30
world religions 600 BCE–600 CE 32

Allegheny
worldwide Christian missions in the early 20th century 36

Almalik
world religions 1500 43

Almaty
Buddhism today 16

Alush
Exodus 18

Alwa
world religions 600 BCE–600 CE 32
world religions 1500 43

Ama-no-Iwato-Jinja
Japan: places of religious importance 50

Amaj
journeys of Muhammad 39

Amalfi
church in 1050 33

Amaravati
early spread of Buddhism 15
Hindu sacred places 10
world religions 600 BCE–600 CE 32

Amarkantak
Hindu sacred places 10

Amarnath
Hindu sacred places 10

Amazon River
Christianity in the Americas c.1750 35

Amida
spread of Islam by 750 CE 40

Amiens
world religions 1500 43

Amisus
Jewish diaspora 21

Amman
Jewish exiles 20
Kingdoms of Saul, David, and Solomon 19

Ammon
Exodus 18
Kingdoms of Saul, David, and Solomon 19

Amoy
worldwide Christian missions in the early 20th century 36

Amravati
Jainism in India 12

Amritsar
modern pilgrimage sites 55
Sikh origins 47
Sikhism in India today 48

Anandpur
Sikh origins 47

Anatu
ancient empire 4

Ancyra
Jewish diaspora 21
spread of Christianity by 325 CE 30

Andhapura
Jainism in India 12

Angkor
early spread of Buddhism 15
world religions 1500 43

Angkor Borai
spread of Islam in South-east Asia 42

Annavaram
Hindu sacred places 10

Anthedon Agrippias
Palestine in the time of Christ 28

Antioch
Christianity in the 4th and 5th centuries 31
Jewish exiles 20
Jews and Christians in the 1st century 29
Jews and Islam 22
Roman religion 6
spread of Christianity by 325 CE 30
spread of Islam by 750 CE 40
world religions 600 BCE–600 CE 32
Zoroastrianism 7

Antioch in Pisidia
Jews and Christians in the 1st century 29

Antipatris
Palestine in the time of Christ 28

Anupshahr
Hindu sacred places 10

Anuradhapura
Buddhism expands in India 14
early spread of Buddhism 15
world religions 600 BCE–600 CE 32

Aparanta
Buddhism expands in India 14

Apollonia
Jews and Christians in the 1st century 29

Aqaba
modern state of Israel 27

Aquileia
Christianity in the 4th and 5th centuries 31
Jewish diaspora 21
spread of Christianity by 325 CE 30

Aquitania
Jewish diaspora 21
spread of Christianity by 325 CE 30

Arabia
Jewish diaspora 21
Jews and Islam 22
world religions 600 BCE–600 CE 32
world religions 1500 43

Arabian desert
journeys of Muhammad 39

Arad
Exodus 18

Arafat (mount)
route of the Hajj 57

Aragon
Reformation Europe 34

Aram-Damascus
Kingdoms of Saul, David, and Solomon 19

Arbela
church in 1050 33
Jewish exiles 20
Zoroastrianism 7

Arbuda
Hindu origins 8

Archelais
Palestine in the time of Christ 28

Arelate
Christianity in the 4th and 5th centuries 31
Jewish diaspora 21
spread of Christianity by 325 CE 30

Areopolis
Palestine in the time of Christ 28

Argos
cult centre 5

Arles
church in 1050 33
see also Arelate

Armagh
  church in 1050 33
Armenia
  Muslim peoples of modern Asia 45
  spread of Christianity by 325 CE 30
  spread of Islam by 750 CE 40
  world religions 600 BCE–600 CE 32
Arnon River
  Exodus 18
Arpad
  Jewish exiles 20
Arvad
  Kingdoms of Saul, David, and
    Solomon 19
Ashdod
  Exodus 18
  Kingdoms of Saul, David, and
    Solomon 19
Ashkelon
  Palestine in the time of Christ 28
Ashur
  ancient empire 4
  Jewish exiles 20
  Mesopotamia 2
Asia
  spread of Christianity by 325 CE 30
Aslone
  spread of Christianity by 325 CE 30
Aspendos
  Jewish exiles 20
Assos
  Jews and Christians in the 1st century
    29
Assyria
  ancient empire 4
  Jewish exiles 20
Asunción
  Christianity in the Americas c.1750 35
Aswan
  Jews and Islam 22
  spread of Islam by 750 CE 40
Athens
  cult centre 5
  Jewish diaspora 21
  Jews and Christians in the 1st century
    29
  Roman religion 6
  spread of Christianity by 325 CE 30
Athos (mount)
  modern pilgrimage sites 55
  world religions 1500 43
Atlanta
  origins of Judaism in the USA 25
Atranjikhera
  Hindu origins 8
Attalia
  Jews and Christians in the 1st century
    29
Auch
  church in 1050 33
Augsburg
  Jews and Islam 223
Augusta Treverorum
  Jewish diaspora 21
  Roman religion 6
  spread of Christianity by 325 CE 30

world religions 600 BCE–600 CE 32
Augustodunum
  Roman religion 6
Auranitis
  Palestine in the time of Christ 28
Auschwitz
  Judaism and the Third Reich 26
Austria
  Judaism in 16th and 17th century
    Europe 23
  Judaism and the Third Reich 26
  New Religious Movements worldwide
    54
  Reformation Europe 34
Austria-Hungary
  Jewish emancipation 24
Ava
  Jewish exiles 20
Avanti
  Buddhism expands in India 14
Avaris
  Ancient Egypt 3
  Exodus 18
Avebury
  megaliths 1
Avignon
  Reformation Europe 34
Axum
  world religions 600 BCE–600 CE 32
  world religions 1500 43
Ayodhya
  Buddhist heartland 13
  Hindu sacred places 10
  world religions 1500 43
Ayutthaya
  world religions 1500 43
Azerbaijan
  Muslim peoples of modern Asia 45
Azotus
  Jews and Christians in the 1st century
    29
  Palestine in the time of Christ 28

Babi-Yar
  Judaism and the Third Reich 26
Babylon
  ancient empire 4
  Jewish diaspora 21
  Jewish exiles 20
  Mesopotamia 2
Babylonia
  Jewish exiles 20
Bactra
  world religions 600 BCE–600 CE 32
  Zoroastrianism 7
Badarika
  Temple Hinduism 9
Badr
  journeys of Muhammad 39
Badrinath
  modern pilgrimage sites 55
Baetica
  Jewish diaspora 21
  spread of Christianity by 325 CE 30

Baghdad
  Jews and Islam 22
  world religions 1500 43
Bahamas
  Christianity in the Americas c.1750 35
Baidyanath
  Hindu sacred places 10
Balanowka
  Judaism and the Third Reich 26
Balfarg
  megaliths 1
Bali
  world religions 1500 43
Balkh
  Jews and Islam 22
  spread of Islam by 750 CE 40
Ballochroy
  megaliths 1
Ballyhoe
  megaliths 1
Baltimore
  Christianity in the Americas c.1750 35
  origins of Judaism in the USA 25
Bandar Labuan
  Taoism 17
Bangalore
  Jainism in India 12
Bangkok
  Buddhism today 16
  Taoism 17
Bangladesh
  Hindu sacred places 10
  Muslim peoples of modern Asia 45
Bangor
  church in 1050 33
Banneux
  modern pilgrimage sites 55
Bantam
  spread of Islam in South-east Asia 42
Bar
  Judaism and the Third Reich 26
Barca
  Jews and Islam 22
  spread of Christianity by 325 CE 30
Barcelona
  Judaism in 16th and 17th century
    Europe 23
  spread of Christianity by 325 CE 30
Barda
  world religions 1500 43
Bargo
  world religions 1500 43
Bari
  church in 1050 33
Barium
  Jewish diaspora 21
Baruch
  Islamic expansion in India 41
Basarh
  Jainism in India 12
Basel
  church in 1050 33
Basra
  Jews and Islam 22

spread of Islam by 750 CE 40
  world religions 1500 43
Basrah
  Buddhist heartland 13
Batanea
  Palestine in the time of Christ 28
Béarn
  Reformation Europe 34
Beaver Island
  Mormon trail 37
Beersheba
  Exodus 18
  Kingdoms of Saul, David, and
    Solomon 19
  modern state of Israel 27
Beijing
  Buddhism today 16
  early spread of Buddhism 15
  Muslim peoples of modern Asia 45
  Taoism 17
  world religions 1500 43
Belgica
  spread of Christianity by 325 CE 30
Belgium
  Jewish emancipation 24
  Judaism and the Third Reich 26
Belgrade
  Reformation Europe 34
Belzek
  Judaism and the Third Reich 26
Benares
  Islamic expansion in India 41
  modern pilgrimage sites 55
Benevento
  church in 1050 33
Berenice
  Jewish diaspora 21
Bergen-Belsen
  Judaism and the Third Reich 26
Berlin
  Judaism in 16th and 17th century
    Europe 23
  Reformation Europe 34
Bernburg
  Judaism and the Third Reich 26
Besor Brook
  Palestine in the time of Christ 28
Beth-Rehob
  Kingdoms of Saul, David, and
    Solomon 19
Beth-shan
  Kingdoms of Saul, David, and
    Solomon 19
Bethany
  Palestine in the time of Christ 28
Bethlehem
  Palestine in the time of Christ 28
  world religions 600 BCE–600 CE 32
Bethphage
  Palestine in the time of Christ 28
Bethsaida
  Palestine in the time of Christ 28
Bhakra
  Sikh origins 47

Bhatinda
Islamic expansion in India 41
Sikh origins 47

Bhilsa
Buddhism expands in India 14

Bhojpur
Hindu sacred places 10

Bhubanesar
Temple Hinduism 9

Bhubaneswar
Hindu sacred places 10
world religions 1500 43

Bialystok
Judaism and the Third Reich 26

Bidar
Islamic expansion in India 41

Bijapuri
Islamic expansion in India 41

Bindhyachal
Hindu sacred places 10

Bi'r Ma'unah
journeys of Muhammad 39

Birzai
Judaism in 16th and 17th century
Europe 23

Bishnupur
Hindu sacred places 10

Bithynia
Jews and Christians in the 1st century
29
spread of Christianity by 325 CE 30

Bitter Lakes
Exodus 18

Black Rock Desert
modern pilgrimage sites 55

Blantyre
worldwide Christian missions in the
early 20th century 36

Bobbio
church in 1050 33

Bodh Gaya
Buddhism expands in India 14
Buddhist heartland 13
early spread of Buddhism 15
modern pilgrimage sites 55
world religions 600 BCE–600 CE 32
world religions 1500 43

Boetia
cult centre 5

Bogdanovka
Judaism and the Third Reich 26

Bogotá
Christianity in the Americas c.1750 35

Bohemia
Reformation Europe 34

Bologna
world religions 600 BCE–600 CE 32

Bombay
worldwide Christian missions in the
early 20th century 36
see also Mumbai

Bonn
Jewish diaspora 21

Bonna
Jewish diaspora 21

Bordeaux
church in 1050 33
Reformation Europe 34

Borneo
spread of Islam in South-east Asia 42
Taoism 17
world religions 600 BCE–600 CE 32
world religions 1500 43

Borobudur
early spread of Buddhism 15
world religions 1500 43

Borsippa
Mesopotamia 2

Boston
Christianity in the Americas c.1750 35
origins of Judaism in the USA 25

Bourges
church in 1050 33
world religions 1500 43

Brahmapura
Islamic expansion in India 41

Brazil
Christianity in the Americas c.1750 35
New Religious Movements worldwide
54

Bremen
church in 1050 33

Brescia
Reformation Europe 34

Breslau
Jewish emancipation 24
Judaism in 16th and 17th century
Europe 23

Brest-Litovsk
Judaism in 16th and 17th century
Europe 23

Brindaban
Hindu sacred places 10

Brindisi
church in 1050 33

Britain
world religions 600 BCE–600 CE 32

Britannia
Christianity in the 4th and 5th
centuries 31
spread of Christianity by 325 CE 30

British Isles
megaliths 1

Brno
Judaism and the Third Reich 26

Broach
Hindu sacred places 10
Zoroastrianism 7

Brodgar (Ring of)
megaliths 1

Brody
Judaism and the Third Reich 26

Brunei
spread of Islam in South-east Asia 42
Taoism 17

Brussels
Reformation Europe 34

Bubastis
Exodus 18

Bucharest
Judaism in 16th and 17th century
Europe 23

Buchenwald
Judaism and the Third Reich 26

Buda
Reformation Europe 34

Budapest
Judaism in 16th and 17th century
Europe 23
Judaism and the Third Reich 26

Bukhara
Islamic expansion in India 41
Jews and Islam 22
spread of Islam by 750 CE 40
world religions 1500 43

Bulgaria
Jewish emancipation 24
Judaism and the Third Reich 26

Burdigala
Roman religion 6

Burhanpur
Islamic expansion in India 41

Busrah
journeys of Muhammad 39

Byblos
Jewish exiles 20

Byzantine empire
journeys of Muhammad 39
world religions 1500 43

Byzantium
Jewish diaspora 21
Roman religion 6
Zoroastrianism 7

Cadiz
Jewish diaspora 21
Jews and Islam 22

Caesarea
Jewish diaspora 21
Jewish exiles 20
Jews and Christians in the 1st century
29
Roman religion 6
world religions 600 BCE–600 CE 32

Caesarea (N. Africa)
Jewish diaspora 21

Caesarea Maritima
Palestine in the time of Christ 28

Caesarea Philippi
Palestine in the time of Christ 28

Cagliari
church in 1050 33

Cairo
Judaism in 16th and 17th century
Europe 23
world religions 1500 43

Calabar
worldwide Christian missions in the
early 20th century 36

Calah
Jewish exiles 20
Mesopotamia 2

Calcutta
worldwide Christian missions in the
early 20th century 36

Calicut
Islamic expansion in India 41

California
origins of Judaism in the USA 25

Callanish
megaliths 1

Cambodia
Buddhism today 16
Taoism 17

Camerino
Reformation Europe 34

Canaan
Exodus 18

Canderi
Islamic expansion in India 41

Canindé
modern pilgrimage sites 55

Canterbury
church in 1050 33
world religions 600 BCE–600 CE 32
world religions 1500 43

Cape Town
worldwide Christian missions in the
early 20th century 36

Capernaum
Palestine in the time of Christ 28

Cappadocia
Jewish diaspora 21
Jews and Christians in the 1st century
29
spread of Christianity by 325 CE 30

Capua, church in 1050 33

Caracas, Christianity in the Americas
c.1750 35

Carales
Roman religion 6
spread of Christianity by 325 CE 30

Carchemish
Jewish exiles 20

Carmel (mount)
Palestine in the time of Christ 28

Carnac
megaliths 1

Carshemish
ancient empire 4

Carthage
Christianity in the 4th and 5th
centuries 31
Roman religion 6
spread of Christianity by 325 CE 30
spread of Islam by 750 CE 40
world religions 600 BCE–600 CE 32

Carthago Nova
Jewish diaspora 21
spread of Christianity by 325 CE 30

Castile
Reformation Europe 34

Castle Rigg
megaliths 1

Castra Regina
Jewish diaspora 21

Cayenne
Christianity in the Americas c.1750 35

Cebu
spread of Islam in South-east Asia 42

Fushima-Imari
    Japan: places of religious importance
        50
Fustate
    Jews and Islam 22
    spread of Islam by 750 CE 40

Galacia
    spread of Christianity by 325 CE 30
Galatia
    Jews and Christians in the 1st century
        29
Galilee
    Palestine in the time of Christ 28
Gallia
    Jewish diaspora 21
    spread of Christianity by 325 CE 30
Gandhara
    Buddhism expands in India 14
    early spread of Buddhism 15
Ganga Sangama
    Hindu origins 8
Gangadvara
    Islamic expansion in India 41
Ganges River
    Buddhism expands in India 14
    Buddhist heartland 13
    early spread of Buddhism 15
    Hindu origins 8
    Hindu sacred places 10
    Islamic expansion in India 41
    Sikh origins 47
    world religions 600 BCE–600 CE 32
Gangotri
    Hindu sacred places 10
    modern pilgrimage sites 55
    world religions 1500 43
Gartok
    world religions 1500 43
Gath
    Kingdoms of Saul, David, and
        Solomon 19
Gaul
    world religions 600 BCE–600 CE 32
Gaulanitis
    Palestine in the time of Christ 28
Gaur
    Islamic expansion in India 41
Gaza
    Exodus 18
    Kingdoms of Saul, David, and
        Solomon 19
    modern state of Israel 27
    Palestine in the time of Christ 28
    spread of Islam by 750 CE 40
Gedes
    Jewish diaspora 21
Gedrosia
    Zoroastrianism 7
Genessaret
    Palestine in the time of Christ 28
Geneva
    Reformation Europe 34
Genoa
    Jewish diaspora 21
    Reformation Europe 34

Georgetown
    Taoism 17
    worldwide Christian missions in the
        early 20th century 36
Georgia
    Muslim peoples of modern Asia 45
    world religions 1500 43
Gerar
    Palestine in the time of Christ 28
Gergesa
    Palestine in the time of Christ 28
Gerizim (mount)
    Palestine in the time of Christ 28
Germania
    Jewish diaspora 21
    spread of Christianity by 325 CE 30
Germany
    Jewish emancipation 24
    Judaism and the Third Reich 26
Ghaghra River
    Buddhism expands in India 14
Ghana
    world religions 1500 43
Ghazni
    Islamic expansion in India 41
    Jews and Islam 22
    spread of Islam by 750 CE 40
    Zoroastrianism 7
Ghor
    Islamic expansion in India 41
Gibeah
    Kingdoms of Saul, David, and
        Solomon 19
Gimar
    Jainism in India 12
Giza
    Ancient Egypt 3
Glasgow
    world religions 1500 43
Glastonbury
    church in 1050 33
    modern pilgrimage sites 55
Gniezno
    church in 1050 33
Goa
    Islamic expansion in India 41
Gokul
    Hindu sacred places 10
Golan Heights
    modern state of Israel 27
Golconda
    Islamic expansion in India 41
Gomateshwara
    Jainism in India 12
Gompa
    world religions 1500 43
Gongxian
    world religions 600 BCE–600 CE 32
Gorakhpur
    Hindu sacred places 10
Gordium
    Zoroastrianism 7
Gortyna
    Roman religion 6

Goshen
    Exodus 18
Gospic
    Judaism and the Third Reich 26
Goulou Shan
    Taoism 17
Gozan
    Jewish exiles 20
Gran
    church in 1050 33
Graz
    Reformation Europe 34
Great Basin
    Mormon trail 37
Great Britain
    Jewish emancipation 24
Greece
    Judaism and the Third Reich 26
Grodno
    Judaism in 16th and 17th century
        Europe 23
Gross Rosen
    Judaism and the Third Reich 26
Guadalupe
    modern pilgrimage sites 55
Guangzhou
    early spread of Buddhism 15
    Muslim peoples of modern Asia 45
    world religions 1500 43
Guatemala
    Christianity in the Americas c.1750 35
Gujarat
    Zoroastrianism 7
Gurs
    Judaism and the Third Reich 26
Gushnasap
    world religions 600 BCE–600 CE 32
Gyantse
    world religions 1500 43

Hadrumetum
    Jewish diaspora 21
    spread of Christianity by 325 CE 30
Haguro-san
    Japan: places of religious importance
        50
Haifa
    modern state of Israel 27
Haiti
    New Religious Movements worldwide
        54
Hajo
    Hindu sacred places 10
Halicz
    Judaism in 16th and 17th century
        Europe 23
Halys River
    Jews and Christians in the 1st century
        29
Hamadan
    Jews and Islam 22
Hamadhan
    spread of Islam by 750 CE 40

Hamath
    ancient empire 4
    Jewish exiles 20
    Kingdoms of Saul, David, and
        Solomon 19
Hamburg
    Judaism in 16th and 17th century
        Europe 23
    Reformation Europe 34
Hami
    world religions 1500 43
Hangzhou
    world religions 1500 43
Hanoi
    early spread of Buddhism 15
    Taoism 17
Hanover
    Reformation Europe 34
Hara
    Jewish exiles 20
Haran
    ancient empire 4
    Jews and Islam 22
Harappa
    Hindu origins 8
Harer
    world religions 1500 43
Haridwar
    Hindu sacred places 10
    modern pilgrimage sites 55
    world religions 1500 43
Harran
    Jewish exiles 20
Haryana
    Sikhism in India today 48
Hattushash
    ancient empire 4
Havana
    Christianity in the Americas c.1750 35
Hazeroth
    Exodus 18
Hazor
    Jewish exiles 20
    Kingdoms of Saul, David, and
        Solomon 19
Hebron
    Exodus 18
    Kingdoms of Saul, David, and
        Solomon 19
    modern state of Israel 27
    Palestine in the time of Christ 28
Heian
    world religions 1500 43
Hejaz
    spread of Islam by 750 CE 40
Helal, Jebel
    Exodus 18
Helicon (mount)
    cult centre 5
Heliopolis
    Ancient Egypt 3
    Exodus 18
Heng
    world religions 600 BCE–600 CE 32

Jirawal
Jainism in India 12

Jiu hua Shan
early spread of Buddhism 15

Jiuquan
world religions 600 BCE–600 CE 32

Johore
spread of Islam in South-east Asia 42

Joppa
Kingdoms of Saul, David, and
Solomon 19
Palestine in the time of Christ 28

Jordan River
Jewish exiles 20
Kingdoms of Saul, David, and
Solomon 19
modern state of Israel 27

Judah
Kingdoms of Saul, David, and
Solomon 19

Judea
Palestine in the time of Christ 28

Juhfa
journeys of Muhammad 39

Julias
Palestine in the time of Christ 28

Julias Livias
Palestine in the time of Christ 28

Jullundur
Sikh origins 47

Juruft
spread of Islam by 750 CE 40

Kabul
Buddhism today 16
Islamic expansion in India 41
Sikh origins 47
spread of Islam by 750 CE 40
Zoroastrianism 7

Kadarnath
Hindu sacred places 10

Kaedsh-barnea
Kingdoms of Saul, David, and
Solomon 19

Kaesong
world religions 600 BCE–600 CE 32

Kaifeng
world religions 1500 43

Kailas (mount)
modern pilgrimage sites 55
world religions 1500 43

Kailasa
Hindu origins 8
Temple Hinduism 9

Kairouan
Jews and Islam 22

Kaiserwald
Judaism and the Third Reich 26

Kalighat
Hindu sacred places 10

Kalika-sangama
Hindu origins 8

Kalinga
Buddhism expands in India 14

Kalinjar
Islamic expansion in India 41

Kalocsa
church in 1050 33

Kalyan
world religions 1500 43

Kamakhya
Hindu sacred places 10

Kanauj
Islamic expansion in India 41

Kanchipuram
early spread of Buddhism 15
Temple Hinduism 9

Kanchpuram
Hindu sacred places 10

Kandahar
Zoroastrianism 7

Kandy
early spread of Buddhism 15
modern pilgrimage sites 55
world religions 600 BCE–600 CE 32

Kangchenjunga
modern pilgrimage sites 55

Kangra
Hindu sacred places 10

Kansas City
Mormon trail 37

Kanya Kumari
Temple Hinduism 9

Kanyakubja
Buddhist heartland 13

Kapilavastu
Buddhist heartland 13

Kapit
Taoism 17

Kar-Tukulti-Ninurta
Mesopotamia 2

Karachi
worldwide Christian missions in the
early 20th century 36

Karbala'
modern pilgrimage sites 55

Karbala
world religions 1500 43

Karkotas
Temple Hinduism 9

Karli
early spread of Buddhism 15
world religions 600 BCE–600 CE 32

Karni Devi
Hindu sacred places 10

Kartarpur
Sikh origins 47

Kashgar
early spread of Buddhism 15
world religions 1500 43

Kashmir
Sikhism in India today 48

Kasi
Temple Hinduism 9

Kaskar
world religions 1500 43

Kasmira
Buddhism expands in India 14

Kasuga
Japan: places of religious importance
50

Katas
Hindu sacred places 10

Kathmandu
Buddhism today 16
modern pilgrimage sites 55

Kaunas
Judaism and the Third Reich 26

Kausambi
Buddhist heartland 13
Hindu origins 8

Kaveri River
Hindu sacred places 10

Kazakhstan
Muslim peoples of modern Asia 45

Kazvin
Jews and Islam 22

Kedara
Temple Hinduism 9

Kedarnath
modern pilgrimage sites 55

Kedesh
Kingdoms of Saul, David, and
Solomon 19

Kells
church in 1050 33

Kerbela
spread of Islam by 750 CE 40

Kerman
Jews and Islam 22

Khaibar
Jews and Islam 22

Khajuraho
Jainism in India 12
Temple Hinduism 9
world religions 1500 43

Khambhat
Islamic expansion in India 41

Khandagiri
Jainism in India 12

Khatu
Hindu sacred places 10

Khaybar
journeys of Muhammad 39

Khetrur
Hindu sacred places 10

Khiva
Jews and Islam 22
world religions 1500 43

Khotan
world religions 600 BCE–600 CE 32

Khyber Pass
Sikh origins 47

Kibroth-hattaavah
Exodus 18

Kiev
Judaism in 16th and 17th century
Europe 23
Judaism and the Third Reich 26
world religions 1500 43

King's Highway
Exodus 18

Kingston
worldwide Christian missions in the
early 20th century 36

Kinnereth
Kingdoms of Saul, David, and
Solomon 19

Kir-hareseth
Kingdoms of Saul, David, and
Solomon 19

Kirkuk
world religions 1500 43

Kirman
spread of Islam by 750 CE 40

Kirtland
Mormon trail 37

Kiryat Shmona
modern state of Israel 27

Kis
Jews and Islam 22

Kish
Mesopotamia 2

Klooga
Judaism and the Third Reich 26

Knock
modern pilgrimage sites 55

Kolhapur
Hindu sacred places 10

Kolkata
Jainism in India 12

Konark
Temple Hinduism 9
world religions 1500 43

Königsberg
Judaism in 16th and 17th century
Europe 23

Konya, world religions 1500 43

Korea
early spread of Buddhism 15
world religions 1500 43

Kosambi
Buddhist heartland 13

Kotipalli
Hindu sacred places 10

Koya-san
Japan: places of religious importance
50

Krakov
Judaism in 16th and 17th century
Europe 23

Krakow
Judaism and the Third Reich 26
Reformation Europe 34

Krishna River
Hindu sacred places 10
Jainism in India 12

K'uai Chi Shan
Taoism 17

Kuala Lumpur
Buddhism today 16
Taoism 17

Kuching
Taoism 17

Kufa
Jews and Islam 22
spread of Islam by 750 CE 40

Kumano
  world religions 1500 43
Kumano-jinja
  Japan: places of religious importance
  50
Kumbum
  world religions 1500 43
Kundalpur
  Hindu sacred places 10
Kunlun
  world religions 600 BCE–600 CE 32
K'uo Ts'ang Shan
  Taoism 17
Kuocang
  world religions 600 BCE–600 CE 32
Kuon-ji
  Japan: places of religious importance
  50
Kuruksetra
  Hindu origins 8
Kusinara
  Buddhist heartland 13
  early spread of Buddhism 15
  world religions 600 BCE–600 CE 32
Kyangui
  early spread of Buddhism 15
Kyongju
  world religions 600 BCE–600 CE 32
  world religions 1500 43
Kyoto
  early spread of Buddhism 15
  Japan: places of religious importance
  50
  world religions 600 BCE–600 CE 32
Kyrgyzstan
  Muslim peoples of modern Asia 45

Lagash
  Mesopotamia 2
Lahore
  Islamic expansion in India 41
  Sikh origins 47
Lal Mandir
  Jainism in India 12
Lalibela
  world religions 1500 43
La Madeleine
  megaliths 1
Lanka
  Hindu origins 8
Lao
  world religions 600 BCE–600 CE 32
Laodicea
  spread of Christianity by 325 CE 30
La Paz
  Christianity in the Americas c.1750 35
Larisa
  Jewish diaspora 21
  spread of Christianity by 325 CE 30
Larsa
  Mesopotamia 2

Latvia
  Judaism and the Third Reich 26
Lauriacum
  Christianity in the 4th and 5th
  centuries 31
Lebanon
  modern state of Israel 27
Leipzig
  Reformation Europe 34
Leon
  church in 1050 33
León
  world religions 1500 43
Leptis Magna
  world religions 600 BCE–600 CE 32
Lérins
  church in 1050 33
Lhasa
  Buddhism today 16
  early spread of Buddhism 15
  modern pilgrimage sites 55
  Taoism 17
  world religions 600 BCE–600 CE 32
  world religions 1500 43
Liaoyang
  world religions 1500 43
Libya
  Jewish diaspora 21
  Jews and Christians in the 1st century
  29
  spread of Christianity by 325 CE 30
  spread of Islam by 750 CE 40
Lima
  Christianity in the Americas c.1750 35
Lincoln
  spread of Christianity by 325 CE 30
  world religions 1500 43
Lindisfarne
  church in 1050 33
Lingjiu
  world religions 600 BCE–600 CE 32
Lios
  megaliths 1
Litani River
  Kingdoms of Saul, David, and
  Solomon 19
Lithuania
  Judaism and the Third Reich 26
  Reformation Europe 34
  world religions 1500 43
Livonia
  Reformation Europe 34
Livorno
  Judaism in 16th and 17th century
  Europe 23
Lodz
  Judaism and the Third Reich 26
Lombok
  spread of Islam in South-east Asia 42
London
  Judaism in 16th and 17th century
  Europe 23
  spread of Christianity by 325 CE 30
Long Meg & daughters
  megaliths 1

Longhu Shan
  Taoism 17
Longmen
  world religions 600 BCE–600 CE 32
Loreto
  modern pilgrimage sites 55
Lorsch
  church in 1050 33
Los Angeles
  Mormon trail 37
  origins of Judaism in the USA 25
Louisiana
  Christianity in the Americas c.1750 35
Louisville
  origins of Judaism in the USA 25
Lourdes
  modern pilgrimage sites 55
Lu
  world religions 600 BCE–600 CE 32
Lu Shan
  Taoism 17
Lublin
  Judaism in 16th and 17th century
  Europe 23
  Judaism and the Third Reich 26
Luck
  Judaism in 16th and 17th century
  Europe 23
Ludhiana
  Sikh origins 47
Ludmir
  Judaism in 16th and 17th century
  Europe 23
Lugdunum
  Jewish diaspora 21
  Roman religion 6
  spread of Christianity by 325 CE 30
Lugo
  church in 1050 33
Lumbini
  Buddhist heartland 13
  early spread of Buddhism 15
  world religions 600 BCE–600 CE 32
Luofou
  world religions 600 BCE–600 CE 32
Luoyang
  early spread of Buddhism 15
  world religions 1500 43
Lusitania
  spread of Christianity by 325 CE 30
Lutetia
  Jewish diaspora 21
Luxembourg
  Judaism and the Third Reich 26
Lvov
  Judaism in 16th and 17th century
  Europe 23
  Judaism and the Third Reich 26
Lycia
  Jews and Christians in the 1st century
  29
Lydda
  Palestine in the time of Christ 28
Lydia
  cult centre 5

Lyon
  Reformation Europe 34
Lyons
  church in 1050 33
  Jewish diaspora 21
Lystra
  Jews and Christians in the 1st century
  29

Maacah
  Kingdoms of Saul, David, and
  Solomon 19
Macassar
  spread of Islam in South-east Asia 42
Macedonia
  Jews and Christians in the 1st century
  29
  spread of Christianity by 325 CE 30
Machaerus
  Palestine in the time of Christ 28
Madedonia
  Jewish diaspora 21
Madras
  Buddhism today 16
  worldwide Christian missions in the
  early 20th century 36
Madura
  spread of Islam in South-east Asia 42
Madurai
  Hindu sacred places 10
  Islamic expansion in India 41
  world religions 1500 43
Magdala
  Palestine in the time of Christ 28
Magdeburg
  church in 1050 33
Maghreb
  Jews and Islam 22
  spread of Islam by 750 CE 40
Magnesia
  cult centre 5
  Jews and Christians in the 1st century
  29
Mahagama
  Buddhism expands in India 14
Mahakuteswar
  Temple Hinduism 9
Mahamadi River
  Buddhism expands in India 14
Maharashtra
  Buddhism expands in India 14
Mahendragiri
  Hindu sacred places 10
Maheshwar
  Hindu sacred places 10
Mahisa Mandala
  Buddhism expands in India 14
Mahismati
  Buddhism expands in India 14
Mahoba
  Hindu sacred places 10
Mahoza
  Jewish exiles 20
Maimana
  Jews and Islam 22

Mainz
  church in 1050 33
  Jewish emancipation 24
Majdanek
  Judaism and the Third Reich 26
Majholi
  Hindu sacred places 10
Makran
  spread of Islam by 750 CE 40
Malacca
  Taoism 17
  world religions 1500 43
  worldwide Christian missions in the early 20th century 36
Malaysia
  Buddhism today 16
Mali
  world religions 1500 43
Mamallapuram
  world religions 1500 43
Manchester
  Mormon trail 37
Mandhata
  Hindu sacred places 10
Mandu
  Islamic expansion in India 41
Mangalagiri
  Hindu sacred places 10
Mangalore
  Hindu sacred places 10
Mangrol
  Hindu sacred places 10
  Islamic expansion in India 41
Manila
  Buddhism today 16
  worldwide Christian missions in the early 20th century 36
Mantua
  Judaism in 16th and 17th century Europe 23
Manzikert
  Christianity in the 4th and 5th centuries 31
Mao
  world religions 600 BCE–600 CE 32
Mao Shan
  Taoism 17
Marah
  Exodus 18
Marakandra
  world religions 600 BCE–600 CE 32
Mari
  ancient empire 4
  Mesopotamia 2
Marmoutier
  world religions 600 BCE–600 CE 32
  Reformation Europe 34
Marseilles
  Jewish diaspora 21
  Reformation Europe 34
  spread of Christianity by 325 CE 30
  world religions 600 BCE–600 CE 32
Maryland
  origins of Judaism in the USA 25

Masad'in Salih
  journeys of Muhammad 39
Mashhad
  modern pilgrimage sites 55
Massachusetts
  origins of Judaism in the USA 25
Massilia
  Jewish diaspora 21
  Roman religion 6
  world religions 600 BCE–600 CE 32
Mathura
  Buddhism expands in India 14
  Buddhist heartland 13
  Hindu origins 8
  Hindu sacred places 10
  Temple Hinduism 9
Mauretania
  Jewish diaspora 21
  spread of Christianity by 325 CE 30
Mauthausen
  Judaism and the Third Reich 26
Mecca
  Jews and Islam 22
  journeys of Muhammad 39
  modern pilgrimage sites 55
  route of the Hajj 57
  spread of Islam by 750 CE 40
  world religions 1500 43
Mechelen
  Judaism and the Third Reich 26
Media
  Jewish exiles 20
Medina
  Jews and Islam 22
  modern pilgrimage sites 55
  spread of Islam by 750 CE 40
  world religions 1500 43
Mediolanum
  Christianity in the 4th and 5th centuries 31
  Jewish diaspora 21
  Roman religion 6
  spread of Christianity by 325 CE 30
Medjugorje
  modern pilgrimage sites 55
Megiddo
  Kingdoms of Saul, David, and Solomon 19
Meiji-jingu
  Japan: places of religious importance 50
Melaka
  spread of Islam in South-east Asia 42
Melbourne
  worldwide Christian missions in the early 20th century 36
Memphis
  Ancient Egypt 3
  ancient empire 4
  Exodus 18
  Jewish diaspora 21
  Roman religion 6
  spread of Christianity by 325 CE 30
  Zoroastrianism 7
Meroë
  Ancient Egypt 3

Merrivale
  megaliths 1
Merry Maidens
  megaliths 1
Merv
  Jews and Islam 22
  spread of Islam by 750 CE 40
Mesopotamia 2
  Jewish exiles 20
  journeys of Muhammad 39
  spread of Christianity by 325 CE 30
  spread of Islam by 750 CE 40
  world religions 600 BCE–600 CE 32
Messene
  Jews and Islam 22
Metz
  Jews and Islam 22
Mexico
  Christianity in the Americas c.1750 35
Miami
  origins of Judaism in the USA 25
Milan
  Christianity in the 4th and 5th centuries 31
  Jewish diaspora 21
  Reformation Europe 34
  Roman religion 6
  spread of Christianity by 325 CE 30
  world religions 1500 43
Miletus
  Jews and Christians in the 1st century 29
Mina
  route of the Hajj 57
Mindanao
  spread of Islam in South-east Asia 42
Minneapolis-St Paul
  origins of Judaism in the USA 25
Minsk
  Judaism in 16th and 17th century Europe 23
  Judaism and the Third Reich 26
Mississippi River
  Christianity in the Americas c.1750 35
  origins of Judaism in the USA 25
Mitanni
  ancient empire 4
Mithila
  Hindu origins 8
Mittelbau Dora
  Judaism and the Third Reich 26
Mitylene
  Jews and Christians in the 1st century 29
Miwa (mount)
  Japan: places of religious importance 50
Moab
  Exodus 18
  Kingdoms of Saul, David, and Solomon 19
Moanhead of Daviot
  megaliths 1
Mocha
  Jews and Islam 22

Modena
  world religions 600 BCE–600 CE 32
Moel Ty Uchaf
  megaliths 1
Moesia
  Jewish diaspora 21
  Jews and Christians in the 1st century 29
Mohenjo-Daro
  Hindu origins 8
  world religions 600 BCE–600 CE 32
Moissac
  church in 1050 33
Moldavia
  Reformation Europe 34
Moluccas
  spread of Islam in South-east Asia 42
Mongolia
  Buddhism today 16
  early spread of Buddhism 15
Monte Cassino
  church in 1050 33
  world religions 600 BCE–600 CE 32
Monterey
  Christianity in the Americas c.1750 35
Montevideo
  worldwide Christian missions in the early 20th century 36
Montserrat
  modern pilgrimage sites 55
Moravia
  Reformation Europe 34
Mosali
  Jainism in India 12
Moschylus (mount)
  cult centre 5
Moscow
  world religions 1500 43
Mostar
  Reformation Europe 34
Mosul
  Jews and Islam 22
  spread of Islam by 750 CE 40
Mount Pisgah
  Mormon trail 37
Muktsar
  Sikh origins 47
Multan
  early spread of Buddhism 15
Mumbai
  Buddhism today 16
  Jainism in India 12
  Zoroastrianism 7
Munich
  Judaism in 16th and 17th century Europe 23
Münster
  Reformation Europe 34
Mursa
  spread of Christianity by 325 CE 30
Musa, Jebel
  Exodus 18
Muscat
  Jews and Islam 22

Mu'ta
  journeys of Muhammad 39
Muzdalifah
  route of the Hajj 57
Myanmar
  Buddhism today 16
  early spread of Buddhism 15
Mycale (mount)
  cult centre 5
Mycenae
  cult centre 5
Mynydd-bach
  megaliths 1
Myra
  Jews and Christians in the 1st century
    29
Mysia
  Jews and Christians in the 1st century
    29
  spread of Christianity by 325 CE 30

Nabadwip
  Hindu sacred places 10
Nabatea
  Palestine in the time of Christ 28
Nablus
  modern state of Israel 27
Nadia
  Islamic expansion in India 41
Nain
  Palestine in the time of Christ 28
Nairanjara River
  Buddhist heartland 13
Najran
  journeys of Muhammad 39
Nalanda
  world religions 1500 43
Nanda Devi (mount)
  modern pilgrimage sites 55
Nanded
  Sikhism in India today 48
Nanhai
  world religions 600 BCE–600 CE 32
Nanjing
  world religions 1500 43
Nankana Sahib
  Sikh origins 47
  world religions 1500 43
Nantes
  Reformation Europe 34
Napata
  Ancient Egypt 3
Naples
  Jewish diaspora 21
  Judaism in 16th and 17th century
    Europe 23
  Reformation Europe 34
  spread of Christianity by 325 CE 30
Nara
  early spread of Buddhism 15
  world religions 1500 43
Narbonensis
  spread of Christianity by 325 CE 30
Narbonne
  church in 1050 33

spread of Christianity by 325 CE 30
Narmada River
  Buddhism expands in India 14
Nasik
  Hindu sacred places 10
Nathdwara
  Hindu sacred places 10
Nauvoo
  Mormon trail 37
Navarre
  Reformation Europe 34
Nazareth
  Palestine in the time of Christ 28
Nazweiler-Struthof
  Judaism and the Third Reich 26
Neapolis
  Jewish diaspora 21
  Palestine in the time of Christ 28
Nebo (mount)
  Exodus 18
Nehavend
  Jewish exiles 20
  spread of Islam by 750 CE 40
Neocaesarea
  church in 1050 33
Nepalearly spread of Buddhism 15
Netherlands
  Judaism in 16th and 17th century
    Europe 23
  Judaism and the Third Reich 26
Neuengamme
  Judaism and the Third Reich 26
New France
  Christianity in the Americas c.1750 35
New Granada
  Christianity in the Americas c.1750 35
New Grange
  megaliths 1
New Jersey
  origins of Judaism in the USA 25
New Orleans
  Christianity in the Americas c.1750 35
  Mormon trail 37
  origins of Judaism in the USA 25
New Spain
  Christianity in the Americas c.1750 35
New York
  Christianity in the Americas c.1750 35
  Mormon trail 37
  origins of Judaism in the USA 25
Newark
  origins of Judaism in the USA 25
Newfoundland
  Christianity in the Americas c.1750 35
Newport
  origins of Judaism in the USA 25
Nicaea
  Christianity in the 4th and 5th
    centuries 31
  world religions 600 BCE–600 CE 32
Nickelsburg
  Judaism in 16th and 17th century
    Europe 23
Nicomedia
  Jewish diaspora 21

Nicopolis
  spread of Christianity by 325 CE 30
Nidaras
  world religions 1500 43
Niederhagen
  Judaism and the Third Reich 26
Nigeria
  New Religious Movements worldwide
    54
Nihawend
  Jews and Islam 22
Nile River
  Ancient Egypt 3
  Christianity in the 4th and 5th
    centuries 31
  Exodus 18
  Jewish diaspora 21
  Jewish exiles 20
  Jews and Christians in the 1st century
    29
  journeys of Muhammad 39
  spread of Christianity by 325 CE 30
  world religions 600 BCE–600 CE 32
Nineveh
  ancient empire 4
  Jewish exiles 20
  Zoroastrianism 7
Nippur
  ancient empire 4
  Jewish exiles 20
  Mesopotamia 2
Nishapur
  Jews and Islam 22
  spread of Islam by 750 CE 40
  world religions 1500 43
Nisibis
  Christianity in the 4th and 5th
    centuries 31
  Jewish diaspora 21
  spread of Christianity by 325 CE 30
  world religions 600 BCE–600 CE 32
  world religions 1500 43
Noë
  Judaism and the Third Reich 26
Noirmoutier
  church in 1050 33
Nola
  world religions 600 BCE–600 CE 32
Noph
  Exodus 18
Noricum
  Jewish diaspora 21
North Korea
  Buddhism today 16
  Taoism 17
Norway
  Jewish emancipation 24
  Judaism and the Third Reich 26
  Reformation Europe 34
Nova Scotia
  Christianity in the Americas c.1750 35
Novgorod
  world religions 1500 43
Noviomagus
  Jewish diaspora 21
Novosibirsk
  Buddhism today 16

Numidia
  Jewish diaspora 21
  spread of Christianity by 325 CE 30
Nuremberg
  Reformation Europe 34
Nuwe
  Ancient Egypt 3

O-mei Shan
  early spread of Buddhism 15
  world religions 600 BCE–600 CE 32
Odessa
  Judaism and the Third Reich 26
Oea
  Jewish diaspora 21
Oescus
  Jewish diaspora 21
Oeta (mount)
  cult centre 5
Olbia
  Jewish diaspora 21
Olives (mount of)
  Jerusalem: holy sites 56
Olympus (mount)
  cult centre 5
Oman
  Muslim peoples of modern Asia 45
Omime-yama
  Japan: places of religious importance
    50
Omkara
  Hindu origins 8
On
  Exodus 18
Ontake-san
  Japan: places of religious importance
    50
Onu
  Ancient Egypt 3
Orontes River
  Kingdoms of Saul, David, and
    Solomon 19
Osaka
  Taoism 17
Osore-yama
  Japan: places of religious importance
    50
Ossa (mount)
  cult centre 5
Ostrog
  Judaism in 16th and 17th century
    Europe 23
Ostrogothic kingdom
  Christianity in the 4th and 5th
    centuries 31
Otranto
  church in 1050 33
Ottoman empire
  Judaism in 16th and 17th century
    Europe 23
  Reformation Europe 34
Oxford
  Reformation Europe 34
Oxus River
  Jews and Islam 22

Roman religion 6
spread of Christianity by 325 CE 30

Sobibor
Judaism and the Third Reich 26

Sofia
Judaism in 16th and 17th century
Europe 23

Somnath
Islamic expansion in India 41
world religions 1500 43

Sonagiri
Jainism in India 12

Song
world religions 600 BCE–600 CE 32

Sonpur
Hindu sacred places 10

Soron
Hindu sacred places 10

Sosnoviec
Judaism and the Third Reich 26

Soumont-St Quentin
megaliths 1

South Africa
New Religious Movements worldwide
54

South Korea
Buddhism today 16
New Religious Movements worldwide
54
Taoism 17

Spain
Jewish emancipation 24
Judaism in 16th and 17th century
Europe 23
Judaism and the Third Reich 26
Reformation Europe 34
spread of Islam by 750 CE 40
world religions 600 BCE–600 CE 32
world religions 1500 43

Sparta
cult centre 5
Jewish diaspora 21
spread of Christianity by 325 CE 30

Split
church in 1050 33

Sravana Belgola
Jainism in India 12

Sri Lanka
Buddhism expands in India 14
Buddhism today 16
early spread of Buddhism 15
world religions 600 BCE–600 CE 32
world religions 1500 43

Sri Pada
modern pilgrimage sites 55

Srinagari
Temple Hinduism 9

Sringeri
Temple Hinduism 9

Sriperumbudur
Temple Hinduism 9

Srirangam
Hindu sacred places 10

Srivijaya
world religions 600 BCE–600 CE 32

Stanleyville
worldwide Christian missions in the
early 20th century 36

Sthanka
world religions 1500 43

Stonehenge
megaliths 1

Strasbourg
world religions 1500 43

Strasburg
Judaism in 16th and 17th century
Europe 23

Strysnow
Judaism and the Third Reich 26

Studion
church in 1050 33

Stutthof
Judaism and the Third Reich 26

Succoth
Exodus 18

Sudan
Muslim peoples of modern Asia 45

Sudji
world religions 1500 43

Suevic kingdom
Christianity in the 4th and 5th
centuries 31

Suhar
spread of Islam by 750 CE 40

Sukothai
early spread of Buddhism 15
world religions 600 BCE–600 CE 32

Sultanpur
Sikh origins 47

Sumatra
early spread of Buddhism 15
spread of Islam in South-east Asia 42
Taoism 17
world religions 600 BCE–600 CE 32
world religions 1500 43

Sumer
Mesopotamia 2

Sung Shan
Taoism 17

Sunium
cult centre 5

Sura
Jewish exiles 20

Surabaya
Buddhism today 16

Suracuse
Jews and Christians in the 1st century
29

Surat
Zoroastrianism 7

Surinam
Christianity in the Americas c.1750 35

Sus
Zoroastrianism 7

Susa
ancient empire 4
journeys of Muhammad 39
Mesopotamia 2

Sutlej River
Hindu origins 8
Sikh origins 47

Sweden
Jewish emancipation 24
Judaism and the Third Reich 26
Reformation Europe 34

Swiss Confederation, Reformation
Europe 34

Switzerland
Jewish emancipation 24
Judaism and the Third Reich 26

Sychar
Palestine in the time of Christ 28

Sydney
worldwide Christian missions in the
early 20th century 36

Syene
Jewish exiles 20

Syracuse
Jewish diaspora 21
Roman religion 6
spread of Christianity by 325 CE 30

Syria
Jewish diaspora 21
Jewish exiles 20
Jews and Christians in the 1st century
29
journeys of Muhammad 39
Muslim peoples of modern Asia 45
Palestine in the time of Christ 28
spread of Christianity by 325 CE 30
spread of Islam by 750 CE 40

Taberah
Exodus 18

Tabor
Mount, Palestine in the time of
Christ 28

Tabriz
Jews and Islam 22

Tabuk
journeys of Muhammad 39
spread of Islam by 750 CE 40

Tadmor
Kingdoms of Saul, David, and
Solomon 19

Tai Shan
modern pilgrimage sites 55

Taibai Shan
Taoism 17

Taichung
Taoism 17

Ta'if
journeys of Muhammad 39

Taima
Jews and Islam 22

Tainan
Taoism 17

Taipei
Buddhism today 16

Taiwan
Buddhism today 16
Taoism 17

Taizé
modern pilgrimage sites 55

Tajikistan
Muslim peoples of modern Asia 45

Tale-yama
Japan: places of religious importance
50

Talwandi
Sikh origins 47

Tamar
Kingdoms of Saul, David, and
Solomon 19

Tamralipti
Buddhism expands in India 14

Tamsui
Taoism 17

Tanais
Jewish diaspora 21

Tangier
spread of Islam by 750 CE 40

Tangut
world religions 1500 43

Tanis
Ancient Egypt 3
Exodus 18
spread of Christianity by 325 CE 30

Tanjavur
Temple Hinduism 9

Tanjore
Islamic expansion in India 41

Tanjungpura
spread of Islam in South-east Asia 42

Tanta
modern pilgrimage sites 55
world religions 1500 43

Tarentum
Jewish diaspora 21

Tarn Taran
Sikh origins 47

Tarnopol
Jewish emancipation 24

Tarraco
Jewish diaspora 21

Tarragona
Jewish diaspora 21
spread of Christianity by 325 CE 30

Tarsus
Christianity in the 4th and 5th
centuries 31
church in 1050 33
Jewish diaspora 21
Jewish exiles 20
Jews and Christians in the 1st century
29

Tashi-gompa
world religions 1500 43

Tashkent
Buddhism today 16
spread of Islam by 750 CE 40

Taxila
Buddhism expands in India 14
early spread of Buddhism 15
Hindu origins 8
world religions 600 BCE–600 CE 32
Zoroastrianism 7

Index

Rome
    ancient 27, 28
    Capitoline Hill 28
    as centre of Christianity 86, 88
    imperial cult 86
    Pantheon 28
Romney, Mitt 103
Rosicrucians 145
Roy, Ram Mohan 40
Russell, Charles Taze 144
Russia 104–5
Russian empire 123
Russian Orthodox Church 92, 105
Rutherford, Joseph 144

Sabarimala temple 41
sacrifice 34, 36
Samuel 62
Sangharakshita 146
Sanskrit 34, 36
Saraswati river 38
Sathya Sai Baba 146
Saturn (god) 25
Saul 62
scholasticism 94
School of Economic Science 147
Scientology 147
Self-Realization Fellowship 146
Serapis 27
Seventh-Day Adventists 144
Shah, Idries 126
Shi'ites 120
Shikoku 134, 148
Shinran 50
Shinto 134

Shiva (god) 36
shop front churches 107
Sikhism 128–31
Sinai 60
Sinai, Mount 60
Smith, Joseph 102–3
Soka Gakkai 146
Solomon 62
Soma (plant god) 34
South America 96
South Korea 99, 106
Soviet Union 104–5
Spain
    as colonial power 96
    conquered by Muslims 68, 112, 120
Sri Lanka 52
Stonehenge 16
Student Volunteer Movement 99
suffering 34, 46
Sufism 116, 120, 123, 124, 126
Sumatra 116
Sumerians 18
sun gods 20
Suzuki, D. T. 146
swamis 146
synagogues 64, 72
syncretism 57
Syria
    ancient 18
    conquered by Muslims 68, 112

Taizé 149
Tajikistan 123
Talmud 68
Tannit 25

Tanta 149
tantras 50
Taoism 56–7, 136
Taylor, James Hudson 98–9
temples 36, 41
    ancient Sumeria 18
    Beijing 56
    Cambodia 52
    Eleusis 26
    Hinduism 36
    Jerusalem 19, 62, 64, 152
    Sikhism 128
Tendai Buddhism 134
Thebes 20
Theravada Buddhism 48
Tibet 50, 52
Tigris river 18
Tours 112
Transcendental Meditation* 146
Travancore 98

UFO religions 147
Ujjain 38
Ukraine, massacre of Jews 70
Ummayad dynasty 112, 113
Unification Church 146
United States of America
    Islam 126–7
    Judaism 74
Unity Church 144
Uranus (sky god) 25
urban civilizations 22
Uruk 18
Utah, Mormons in 102–3
Utu (sun god) 18
Uzbekistan 123

Varanasi 38
Varuna (sea god) 40
Vedanta Society 146
Vedas 34
Vikvekananda (Swami) 40
Vipassana movement 146
Vishnu (god) 36
Vivekananda (swami) 146
Vorihon, Claude 147
Vulcan (god of war) 25

Waihind 114
Walsingham 149
Wang Yang-ming 54
White, Ellen G. 144
Wise, Isaac 74
writing 18

Xavier, Francis 98

Yamuna river 38
Yavneh 67
Yiddish 70
yoga 35
Yogananda, Paramahansa 146
Young, Brigham 102–3

Zen 50, 146
Zeus 25, 28
Zevi, Shabbetai 70
Zionism 78
Zoroastrianism 30, 113
Zwingli, Huldrych 94